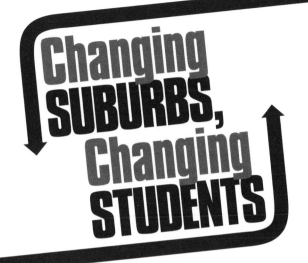

Changing SUBURBS, Changing STUDENTS

A prime function of a leader is to keep hope alive.
(John W. Gardner, Secretary of Health, Education, and Welfare
1968 [1912–2002])
To our loved ones,
who keep us grounded and hopeful each and every day of our lives.

From SBW: To my husband Roy Wepner; and daughters, sons-in-law, and
grandchildren—Meredith, Judd, and Eliza Grossman; Leslie, Marc, and
Teddy Regenbaum—for their unconditional love and support.

From JF: In memory of my parents, Marie and Rosario Barbato, and in grati-
tude for the ongoing support of my husband Frank Ferrara and daughters,
Francesca and Therésé.

From KR: To my son, Joseph (Joey) DeSabia III, whose curiosity and wonder
helps me to see everything anew.

From DWG: To my husband and best friend, David; daughters—Cristina,
Julia and Victoria; and parents, Stanley and Ethel Wickham
por sus consejos, apoyo y amor. Los adoro. (for your advice,
support and love. I adore you.)

From DEL: To my mother, Mary Ann Lang, for teaching me that there are
many ways to see every situation and supporting me as a writer.

From LB: To my mother Yvonne Bigaouette for past and ongoing
support of my literary projects; and for the invaluable
support and friendship of LG.

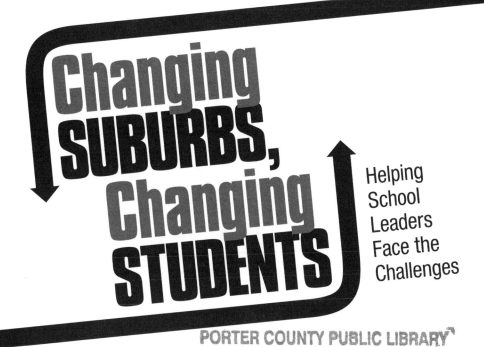

Changing SUBURBS, Changing STUDENTS

Helping School Leaders Face the Challenges

SHELLEY B. WEPNER

and the

CHANGING SUBURBS INSTITUTE®

JoAnne Ferrara, Kristin N. Rainville, Diane W. Gómez, Diane E. Lang, and Laura Bigaouette

Foreword by Sonia Nieto

CORWIN
A SAGE Company

CORWIN
A SAGE Company

FOR INFORMATION:

Corwin
A SAGE Company
2455 Teller Road
Thousand Oaks, California 91320
(800) 233-9936
www.corwin.com

SAGE Publications Ltd.
1 Oliver's Yard
55 City Road
London, EC1Y 1SP
United Kingdom

SAGE Publications India Pvt. Ltd.
B 1/I 1 Mohan Cooperative Industrial Area
Mathura Road, New Delhi 110 044
India

SAGE Publications Asia-Pacific Pte. Ltd.
3 Church Street
#10–04 Samsung Hub
Singapore 049483

Acquisitions Editor: Debra Stollenwerk
Associate Editor: Desirée A. Bartlett
Editorial Assistant: Kimberly Greenberg
Production Editor: Cassandra Margaret Seibel
Copy Editor: Rickye Reber
Typesetter: Hurix Systems Pvt. Ltd.
Proofreader: Caryne Brown
Indexer: Wendy Allex
Cover Designer: Gail Buschman
Permissions Editor: Adele Hutchinson

Printed in the United States of America.

Library of Congress Cataloging-in-Publication Data

Wepner, Shelley B., 1951– author.

Changing suburbs, changing students : helping school leaders face the challenges / Shelley B. Wepner, JoAnne Ferrara, Kristin N. Rainville, Diane W. Gomez, Diane E. Lang, Laura Bigaouette ; Foreword by Sonia Nieto.

pages cm

Includes bibliographical references and index.

ISBN 978-1-4522-0391-1 (paperback)

1. Suburban schools—United States—Administration. 2. Suburban teenagers—Education—United States. 3. Education, Secondary—United States. 4. Educational leadership—United States.
I. Title.

LC5145.2.W46 2012

373.09173'3—dc23

2012020443

This book is printed on acid-free paper.

12 13 14 15 16 10 9 8 7 6 5 4 3 2 1

Contents

List of Figures

Foreword

The suburb—that quintessentially American invention—has generally conjured up images of cul-de-sacs in peaceful tree-lined neighborhoods, comfortable modern homes populated overwhelmingly by white, middle-class, English-speaking, two-parent families with two children, a dog, and a cat. Suburbs also recall images of children selling lemonade, fathers mowing lawns, and mothers preparing picnics. Yet such ubiquitous images, made popular through the media over the past half century or more, are little more than romantic and idyllic views far from the reality of many modern suburbs.

Suburbs are changing, as the authors of this book make abundantly clear, and the population of the children in suburban schools is also changing, sometimes at a dramatic pace. There are many reasons for this change: Suburban sprawl leading to blurred boundaries between cities and suburbs; the eternal quest of families to escape cities for more peaceful and less chaotic daily living, as well as their search for better schools for their children; and, most of all, the changing demographics of the nation as a whole.

It is by now a well-known fact that whites will become a minority in the United States in another three decades. While the populations of African Americans, Asian Americans, American Indians, and immigrants from all over the world have all steadily increased in the past half century, the population of whites has decreased in proportion. The case of Latinos especially, that is people originally from Mexico, the Caribbean, and Central and South America, is particularly striking. The Latino population, the largest group of people from diverse backgrounds in the nation since 2000, has grown exponentially during this same time; this change is evident not only in schools but also, for example, in the *bodegas* and *taquerias* and other businesses that prominently display their wares and services in Spanish. If this is the case, we should expect these population shifts to occur not just in urban areas but also in small towns, rural areas, and suburbs. That is precisely what is happening, and many schools have been caught unprepared.

In *Changing Suburbs, Changing Students,* Shelley Wepner and the Changing Suburbs Institute provide a valuable resource for school leaders who are facing these changes, and even for those who realize the change is coming but have not yet experienced it. With vignettes, case studies, and practical strategies, this book addresses such significant issues as how to meet the needs of students for whom English is a second or additional language, how to work effectively with families who are unfamiliar with—and many times uncomfortable with—the U.S. educational system, and how to provide meaningful professional development for teachers who are often at a loss when facing a changing student body. School leaders will turn to this book frequently in their search to provide an excellent education to all students, not simply to the traditional residents of suburbs but to their newer members as well.

As Shelley and her colleagues make clear, making way for the new students and families in our suburban schools requires not superficial changes or tinkering around the edges of the system while keeping in place old ideas, policies, and practices. Instead, what is required is a complete overhaul of previous policies, programs, and practices that, while they might have been successful in the past, may no longer be adequate for the changing times. That is, changing suburbs requires a transformation in the very culture and climate of schools to make them more open and welcoming spaces accessible to all students and their families.

Experience tells us that change cannot be mandated. We cannot make school leaders, community members, or teachers automatically welcome with open arms new students in our changing suburbs. Authentic transformation takes hard work, careful planning, and thoughtful collaboration. But through such initiatives as the Changing Suburbs Institute, a climate can be created that supports the development of attitudes that value student differences and actions that help transform schools. What is most needed to make suburban schools places of excellence for all students is a change of perspective in the minds and hearts of the policymakers, administrators, and teachers in suburban schools. This means moving from a deficit perspective that views students of diverse backgrounds as problems and impediments to successful schools to viewing them as valued resources who can enrich the schools and all who inhabit them. Rather than viewing the fact that students might not speak English, a resource perspective views them as, for example, Spanish speakers who are on their way to becoming bilingual. Rather than viewing the families of the new children in suburban schools as ignorant and uncaring (a frequent but unfortunate and incorrect characterization by some school personnel), a resource perspective means viewing them as people who have many talents and resources to bring to the schools and as valuable allies in the education of their children.

The authors of this book remind us that all children are worthy of an excellent education and that it is up to school leaders and teachers to think of the students in their changing schools as opportunities, as possibilities, and even as a joy. Only in this way will our schools—urban, suburban, and rural—be places where the American ideal of a free, public, and excellent education is available to all. Our children deserve no less.

Sonia Nieto

Preface

Rationale for Writing *Changing Suburbs, Changing Students: Helping School Leaders Face the Challenges*

There is a new reality in suburban school districts, and suburban school leaders need ideas and strategies for addressing their changing student population. This book was written to help suburban school leaders address their new reality. Suburban schools are changing as a result of an increasingly diverse student population, particularly with English language learners (ELLs). These changes are the result of changes in the suburbs, which are no longer just white, middle-class enclaves with predominately white students attending exemplary schools. Many suburban areas resemble urban neighborhoods where unemployment, overcrowded housing, poverty, crime, and mobility exist. These new suburban challenges affect schools and student achievement. The achievement gap between the haves and the have-nots in changing suburban schools has become the focal point of this new reality and needs to be dealt with strategically, steadily, competently, and financially.

Unfortunately, politicians and legislators who influence the level of funding that goes into schools focus on the achievement gap in urban schools and the urgency of pouring more money and resources into such schools. They do not recognize that many of the urban needs now are suburban needs, which makes it that much more difficult for suburban school leaders to have the funds needed to work with teachers and students to begin to close the ever-growing achievement gap.

Part of the problem for suburban school leaders has been the gradual and easy-to-ignore demographic shifts in their communities (Louis, 2003). There has also been a problem with school leaders' need to balance a changing student population with an increasingly high-stakes environment (Crow, 2006). Suburban school leaders have to be responsive to a high-stakes testing environment and to their own increasingly diverse settings. Unlike school leaders in high-poverty urban schools who know what to expect in assuming such positions, school leaders in changing suburban districts are encountering something different from what they initially envisioned. Their once-white, high-achieving, good schools and districts now are fraught with issues related to achievement, discipline, and despair. The time has come to put a spotlight on the challenges of changing suburban school districts so that school leaders can address student achievement challenges thoughtfully and proactively.

Audience and Purpose

This book is written for practicing and prospective superintendents, assistant superintendents, principals, assistant principals, curriculum directors, and master's and doctoral students in leadership and curriculum programs who work in or intend to work in a suburban school district that is becoming increasingly diverse. Unlike any other book on the market, this book discusses and describes

- Ways to think about and adjust to the changes in suburban school districts to accommodate the needs of an increasingly diverse student population, especially ELLs
- New ideas and strategies for addressing the changing culture of their suburban schools and working effectively with teachers, students, and their parents
- Visionary leadership practices for forming partnerships and developing community schools to help teachers develop professionally and help students achieve in changing suburban schools

This book's purpose is to help suburban school leaders serve as change agents in dealing with the cultural and political changes in their schools. School leaders need to be able to recognize and address ways in which their actions, behaviors, and decisions affect how their schools work with students from diverse backgrounds. This is especially significant when 88 percent of the nation's principals are white and 90 percent of the nation's teachers are white, middle class, and English speaking (Evans, 2007; Howard, 2007).

Increased student diversity puts a strain on suburban teachers and other staff members who often are from different socioeconomic backgrounds than their low-income minority students. School leaders can help teachers be more culturally sensitive to students' needs and learning styles, offer appropriate educational services, provide on-site social services, monitor students' instructional progress, and develop new curricula that help students thrive in this era of high-stakes testing (Crow, 2006; Louis, 2003). This book explores options for school leaders to use so they can provide the best possible environment for their changing student population. While many of the ideas and strategies could be used by leaders in urban and rural districts as well, they are written for suburban school leaders who must contend with an achievement gap that is now both obvious and disconcerting.

Conceptual Framework for the Book

We discovered the urgency of attending to changes in suburban school districts when one of us met with a potential donor to our college in 2005. This donor wondered why we were focused on urban education issues when in her mind the suburbs surrounding the college were faced with some of the same problems as the urban districts. She was watching her own suburban town change before her eyes and knew that the schools were having difficulty adjusting to these changes. She asked, "Are you aware of the challenges that the school leaders in your surrounding school districts are experiencing? Are you preparing your teachers for these changing districts?" It was at that point that we realized that we needed to do something about and with our surrounding changing school districts.

We came up with the concept of the Changing Suburbs Institute (CSI) in recognition of the increasing diversity in suburban school districts and the need to ensure that currently practicing and prospective teachers are prepared to teach an increasingly diverse student population. We determined that our focus would be on Hispanic students because our surrounding suburban districts had the most increase in the Hispanic population. However, the concept can be applied to any diverse student population. We conducted research on the demographics of the changing suburbs; searched thoroughly for existing publications about the changing suburbs; worked regularly with school leaders, teachers, and students in changing suburban schools; and interacted with parents, especially new immigrants, to try to figure out how to best address the myriad of issues that had emerged. Unlike the TV show *CSI*, we know that we cannot find one answer to the challenges of the changing suburbs. But as on *CSI*, we can use our painstakingly hard work, creative wit, persistence, and team effort to discover new and useful clues on what has potential for promoting learning for our changing student population.

Components of the Changing Suburbs Institute

The CSI focuses on four major areas: (1) teacher and school leadership development, (2) collaboration, (3) parent education, and (4) dissemination of information. Figure P.1 provides a graphic depiction of CSI's components.

To address teacher and school leadership development, we established professional development schools (PDSs) in our CSI school districts. Each district has had at least a 7 percent increase in Hispanic students in the last four years. The PDSs focus on the professional development of teachers, teacher candidate preparation, student learning, and practitioner inquiry. Our college provides to each school a PDS liaison who is employed by the college and works at the PDS at least two days each week to serve as a conduit between the school and the college. PDS liaisons work primarily with practicing teachers and teacher candidates to support their development so that they in turn can enhance student learning. Consultants and other college faculty also engage with PDS teachers and students to support teaching and learning. Each PDS pays a fee to the college to be part of the network. Our college currently has eight PDSs: six elementary schools, one middle school, and one high school.

Each PDS has a leadership team that develops programs, projects, and opportunities for the school, for example, reading and writing workshops in which college faculty work directly with PDS teachers to help them modify instructional practices; during- and after-school tutoring programs in mathematics and reading to help students with test preparation; a teacher mentoring program in which classroom teachers serve as mentors for new teachers; a teacher intern program for graduate students who become employed by the district to serve in a combination of roles (yearlong substitute teachers, teaching assistants, tutors, and before- and after-school program facilitators); and a teaching fellows program to enable teacher candidates to spend all of their fieldwork in one school over a two-year period so that they can

Figure P.1   Changing Suburbs Institute (CSI)

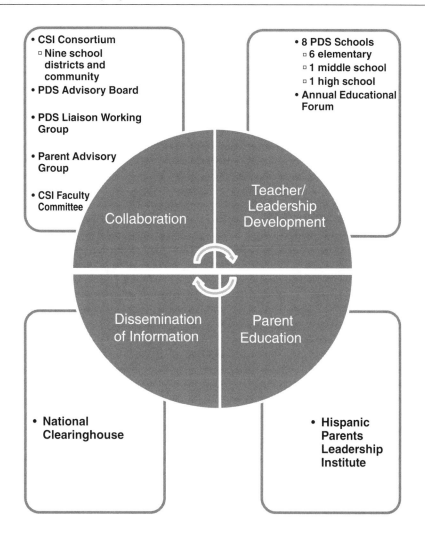

assist teachers and students in the school. These projects and programs are used with all students irrespective of their racial, ethnic, cultural, or linguistic background.

The PDSs provide placements for field experiences and student teaching and are entitled to special discounts for the teaching staff for coursework, conferences, and special events. One of the earliest PDSs has hired our college's graduates for one-third of its teaching staff. The PDS students participate in a special college visitation day to learn about the academic and extracurricular benefits of attending college because many of these students would be the first in their family to attend college. High school students from a PDS district who are accepted to our college are entitled to a 50 percent tuition discount for all four undergraduate years if they maintain a satisfactory grade point average.

A PDS Advisory Board—comprised of the eight PDS principals, eight PDS liaisons, and Manhattanville College faculty and administrators—meet at least two times each year to exchange ideas, develop goals, and assess progress within and across schools. A PDS Liaison Working Group—comprised of the eight PDS liaisons and Manhattanville administrators and staff—meet monthly to discuss each school's progress and challenges. This group also collects and analyzes data across the eight schools about the PDSs' impact. So far, the data have indicated changes in teachers' instructional methodologies, changes in teacher candidates' level of confidence for first-time teaching, changes in students' achievement and attitudes toward learning, and increases in action research by teachers.

The CSI also holds an annual educational forum that brings renowned experts as keynote speakers to present current research about and practices for working effectively with diverse student populations. Workshop presenters showcase accomplishments in CSI school districts and help attendees develop new insights about Hispanic students' culture, background, behavior, and immigration experiences.

To address collaboration, CSI formed a consortium of school leaders, teachers, and community members. The consortium meets bimonthly to provide networking opportunities and share best practices. This sharing has resulted in the implementation of new programs in CSI school districts, such as a Newcomer's Center for Hispanic students and families and the establishment of programs for ELLs. In addition to the other collaborative committees identified in Figure P.1, CSI has a CSI Faculty Committee that develops and implements short- and long-term goals, and plans the annual educational forum.

To address parent education, CSI offers an annual Hispanic Parents Leadership Institute to help parents learn about the U.S. educational system so that they can become more involved in their children's education. Immigrants new to the United States are included in this parent group. A committee of CSI school leaders, guidance counselors, social workers, and community organizers plan the institute and determine program strategy.

To address dissemination of information, a clearinghouse was developed to serve as a public resource about the composition and complexity of the changing suburbs and mechanisms for creating changes in schools. The clearinghouse provides information about the challenges and successes in meeting the needs of diverse student populations, especially ELLs, and selected programs, research studies, and instructional methodologies. Because the college's newly established doctoral program in educational leadership has as its theme the changing suburbs and small cities, doctoral dissertations related to this theme are scheduled to be included in this clearinghouse. The clearinghouse can be found at http://www.mville.edu/graduate/academics/education/about/changing-suburbs-instituter/clearinghouse.html.

Although initiated by a college, CSI is working because it is a grassroots, collaborative approach to identifying programs, projects, and people to help with a growing minority student population in the suburbs. There are thirteen different and unique teams of school-based, university-based, and community-based leaders and teachers who get together to focus on a specific task or initiative related to helping the changing student and parent population better acclimate to school expectations.

The ideas, examples, and promising practices included in this book are a result of our direct work with the school leaders, teachers, students, and community leaders working and living in our CSI districts, yet these same strategies can apply to any district that is changing or needs to address student achievement challenges.

Contents of the Book

The first part of the book discusses the changing suburbs and the role of school leaders—superintendents and principals—in addressing the challenges of such change. The second part provides specific ideas for school leaders about changing the culture of the school, providing professional development for teachers, implementing programs for diverse student populations, forming school–university collaborations, and working with parents to help develop people and programs in changing suburban school districts. The efforts and outcomes of CSI are mentioned throughout the book as examples of successful strategies.

Part I: The Challenges of Changing Suburban School Districts

Part I presents an overview about changing suburban school districts and their impact on school leaders. Chapter 1 discusses the concept and demographics of the changing suburbs and the implications of such changes on schools and school leaders. Chapter 2 describes what superintendents and principals can do to meet the needs of the community in light of national, statewide, and local mandates.

Part II: Addressing the Challenges of Changing Suburban School Districts

Part II delves into ways to change the culture of a changing suburban school, provide professional development for teachers, implement programs for diverse student populations, create school–university collaborations, and work with parents. Chapter 3 describes ways in which school leaders can change their schools and districts and presents specific classroom examples with tools to use and guidelines for such changes. Chapter 4 discusses the role of the school leader in providing professional development and provides ideas on how to offer relevant, useful professional development to teachers experiencing changes with their student population. Chapter 5 discusses what school leaders need to know in identifying, implementing, and assessing programs to meet the needs of diverse student populations. Chapter 6 provides an overview of the benefits and challenges of school–university partnerships and offers guidelines for developing such partnerships. Chapter 7 describes how an elementary school in a changing suburban district evolved from a low-achieving, low-morale school to a high-achieving, highly engaged school that is now showcased as a school of excellence because of its transformation into a community school. Chapter 8 discusses the differing needs and issues of parents in changing suburban school districts and provides general and specific ideas and guidelines for involving parents in the schools to promote student achievement.

The book closes with a summary of guidelines for school leaders so all the guidelines presented across the chapters are in one place to facilitate school leaders' ability to develop their own new strategies for effecting change.

Unique Features of the Book

- Vignettes in the beginning of each chapter and within chapters that describe situations related to the chapter topic: These vignettes describe real-life, school-based situations that have occurred in changing suburban schools to highlight what school leaders have done, could do, or should at least consider doing.

- Examples of successful classroom practices in changing suburban schools with recommended tools for implementing changes: These practices provide insight into what other school leaders have done so that they can be adopted or adapted in other districts.
- Guidelines in the last section of every chapter for school leaders to consider: These guidelines provide specific and concrete ideas for looking at the district as a whole, changing the culture of the schools, implementing programs, working with teachers and parents, and reaching out to the community to bring the necessary resources to the schools.

We invite you to join us in our journey of discovering and addressing the many challenges of the changing suburban school districts so that together we can bring to the forefront a new reality that has yet to be fully appreciated by those with financial and political influence.

Acknowledgments

We gratefully acknowledge those who have helped us weave together our experiences and ideas into a book about the new realities for school leaders. Everyone involved with this publication challenged us to think globally as we acted locally and argue persuasively as we wrote concretely.

Our publishing story began when Debra Stollenwerk, Senior Acquisitions Editor at Corwin, called Shelley to have a conversation about what we meant by the *changing suburbs*. She knew what she was experiencing in her region in Ohio and wanted to know whether what she saw was consistent with what we saw. She previously had spoken with local administrators and knew that they were grappling with the same issues in trying to adequately address diverse student needs as a result of shifting demographics. She realized that the notion of the changing suburbs had become such a pressing issue for school leaders and their teachers that a book needed to be written to bring the topic to the forefront. Debra then worked carefully and tirelessly with Shelley to develop a focused purpose and general outline. We appreciate Debra's support to promote the concept on a national scale.

A prelude to this story is a conversation that Carol Chambers Collins, former Senior Acquisitions Editor at Corwin, had with Shelley about pitching the concept. Carol knew Shelley previously in life and, thankfully for us, thought that the idea would work well for the administration and leadership focus of the company. We are indebted to Carol for introducing us to Debra.

The heart and soul of this book comes from the school leaders who have been quietly and painstakingly handling their changing suburban challenges with their teaching and administrative staff. Those mentioned in this book represent the many school leaders who have played major roles in addressing head-on the myriad of issues that have arisen as a result of changing demographics: Annemarie Berardi, Principal of Fox Lane Middle School in Bedford, New York; Lenora Boehlert, Assistant Superintendent for Human Resources of White Plains School District in New York, New York; Marguerite Clarkson, Principal of R.J.

Bailey School in Greenburgh 7, New York; George Crute, Lead Teacher for Professional Development for Bedford School District in Bedford, New York; Mimi Donovan, Principal of Galloway Ridge Intermediate School in Columbus, Ohio; Felix Flores, former Principal of Claremont School in Ossining, New York; Maria Flores, Community School Coordinator for Edison Community School in Port Chester, New York; Jere Hochman, Superintendent of Bedford School District in Bedford, New York; Kimmerly Nieves, Principal of Jefferson Elementary School in New Rochelle, New York; Richard Organisciak, Superintendent of the New Rochelle City School District in New Rochelle, New York; Eileen Santiago, Former Principal of Thomas A. Edison School in Port Chester, New York; Cynthia Slotkin, Former Principal of Jefferson Elementary School, New Rochelle, New York; Rosa Taylor, Principal of the Park Avenue School in Port Chester, New York; and Zoila Tazi, Principal of the Park Early Childhood Center in Ossining, New York.

Thank you to the classroom teachers who allowed us to pick their brains and test our theories about ways to address their changing classrooms: Corey Andrews, Stephanie Arrington, Terri DeLorenzo, Sandra DeSillas, and Tina Guzzetti, all from the New Rochelle School District in New Rochelle, New York.

Other individuals who played critical roles in publishing this book include Ross Collin, Assistant Professor of Literacy in the School of Education at Manhattanville College, who facilitates an action-research group at a PDS and shared their stories; Lynda Hanley, Education Librarian at Manhattanville College, who helped with research and citations; Stephanie Jones, University of Georgia, Kristin's mentor and friend whose collaborations influenced her contributions to the book; and Kate Rogan, graduate assistant at Manhattanville College, who was enormously helpful in scouring the literature to find whatever was written about changing suburban districts and the role of school leaders in addressing this newfound challenge.

We and Corwin thank the reviewers of our first draft for giving us critically important feedback and extremely useful recommendations for strengthening the way in which we present our message, describe ideas, and offer examples for both district and school leaders:

Kenneth M. Arndt, Superintendent
Community Unit School District 300
Carpentersville, Illinois

Martin J. Hudacs, Superintendent
Solanco School District
Quarryville, Pennsylvania

Steve Hutton, Superintendent
Beechwood Independent Schools
Ft. Mitchell, Kentucky

Susan N. Imamura, Retired Principal
Manoa Elementary School
Honolulu, Hawaii

Linda Jungwirth, President,
Convening Conversations, Inc.
Pepperdine University
Los Angeles, California

Beth Madison, Principal
Robert Gray Middle School
Portland, Oregon

Jacie Maslyk, Principal
Crafton Elementary
Pittsburgh, Pennsylvania

Tanna H. Nicely, Assistant Principal
Dogwood Elementary
Knoxville, Tennessee

Belinda J. Raines, Principal
Northwestern High School
Detroit, Michigan

We also thank the Corwin staff for their unusual kindness and helpfulness. Kimberly Greenberg set the stage for preparing our manuscript, while Cassandra Margaret Seibel and Rickye Reber oversaw the production of our manuscript. Their sharp eyes, keen sense of style, and impressive knowledge of the English language transformed our manuscript into a crisply written and visually appealing publication.

Finally, and personally most important, we thank our families and friends for their patience with our distractibility, absence from activities, delinquent behaviors with daily responsibilities, and overall inability to attend to life's events. Their magnanimity in giving us time and space to write is forever appreciated.

About the Authors

Shelley B. Wepner is Dean and Professor of Education in the School of Education at Manhattanville College in Purchase, New York. She was a K–12 teacher and administrator for nine years in three districts in New Jersey before becoming a faculty member and administrator in higher education. Prior to her position at Manhattanville College, she was a faculty member and administrator at William Paterson University in Wayne, New Jersey, and Widener University in Chester, Pennsylvania. At both institutions, she worked with her local principals and superintendents to form school–university partnerships and develop professional development schools at the elementary, middle school, and high school levels. Her vested interest in working with school leaders in changing suburban school districts comes from her involvement with the Changing Suburbs Institute, which she and her colleagues created to address the professional development and student achievement needs of the surrounding school districts and the teacher preparation needs of her college. She also worked with her colleagues to seek approval for a doctoral program in educational leadership focused on the changing suburbs. She has published over 130 articles, book chapters, software packages, and books, which are most recently related to connections between K–12 education and higher education and leadership skills for effectively supporting teacher education and literacy development. Her most recent coedited books are *The Administration and Supervision of Reading Programs*, 4th edition, and *Collaborative Leadership in Action: Partnering for Success in Schools*, both published by Teachers College Press. She received her EdD from the University of Pennsylvania.

    JoAnne Ferrara is Associate Dean for Undergraduate Admissions and Advising, Chair of the Department of Curriculum and Instruction, and PDS Coordinator in the School of Education at Manhattanville College. She has served as an elementary school teacher in both general and special education settings. In addition to her classroom experience, she spent several years as a school administrator for the New York City Department of Education. In 2002, she founded the School of Education's first professional development school in a changing suburban school in Westchester County, New York. She strongly believes in the power of school–university partnerships to provide teacher education candidates with authentic experiences in classrooms, while providing classroom teachers with job-embedded professional development opportunities. For more than a decade, Dr. Ferrara has been investigating the ways in which professional development schools situated within community schools support teacher education. Dr. Ferrara presents regularly at state and national conferences. Her research interests and publications focus primarily on professional development schools, whole-child education, community schools, and new teacher induction. Recent publications focus on using partnerships to prepare elementary teachers for the changing suburbs, preparing preservice teachers to support the needs of the whole child, and developing a unique focus to a PDS. She received her EdD from Nova Southeastern University.

Kristin N. Rainville is Assistant Professor and Chair of the Literacy Department in the School of Education at Manhattanville College. Kristin also worked as a PDS liaison at an elementary school in a changing suburb. As the liaison, Kristin worked collaboratively with faculty and administration to examine and strengthen teaching practices, empower students and families, and prepare new teachers. Kristin is a former elementary classroom teacher, literacy coach, and state-level program coordinator. Kristin's research and writing focus is on literacy leadership, whether through literacy coaching, classroom instruction, action research, or teacher candidate preparation. Kristin has published on literacy coaching and is currently working on a project investigating the power of field-based literacy methods courses and the professional learning of the classroom teachers who host and cofacilitate the courses. Kristin works with districts and schools in New York, New Jersey, and Connecticut, supporting them as they strengthen their literacy curriculum, teaching, and learning. Kristin continually presents at local, national, and international conferences. Kristin received her EdD from the Teachers College at Columbia University, where she was an instructor.

Diane W. Gómez is Chair of the Department of Educational Leadership and Special Subjects and Assistant Professor for Second Languages in the School of Education at Manhattanville College. Diane is a former high school Spanish teacher and has taught English as a Second Language (ESL) and students with special needs. She works closely with teachers, parents, and administrators and offers teacher candidates pragmatic skills with theoretical foundations. As a PDS liaison for a CSI partnership school and member of CSI, she is a strong proponent of bilingual education. Her research interests include multicultural education in field-based settings, literacy in the context of dual language, and second language programs. She is a frequent presenter at local, national, and international conferences, often copresenting with CSI colleagues Diane Lang and JoAnne Ferrara. She has published articles and book chapters on topics related to the CSI mission and second language learners. Her most recent publication is a collaborative chapter with colleague JoAnne Ferrara about their CSI school district's commitment to full-service community schools in *Breaking the Mold of Education for Culturally and Linguistically Diverse Students: Innovative and Successful Practices for 21st Century Schools, Volume III*, published by Rowman & Littlefield. She received her PhD from Fordham University in language literacy and learning.

Diane E. Lang is Director of Instructional Support Services for the Orange-Ulster Board of Cooperative Educational Services (OU BOCES) in Goshen, New York. Previously, she was an Associate Professor of Early Childhood and Childhood Education at Manhattanville College, where she was a PDS liaison at a CSI partnership school and taught field-based methodology courses in curriculum, assessment and management, social studies, and mathematics. With a research focus on immigrant children and schooling, she has published, presented, and consulted on modeling and supporting home-based literacy strategies with Hispanic parents, school-based outreach to immigrant families, and teaching social studies in diverse educational settings. Her recent publications have focused on improving the teaching of social studies and science and supporting parents to engage in culturally and linguistically diverse schools. She was a school administrator and elementary teacher in New York City and Westchester County, New York. Interested in culture and learning at an early age, she began her career in education serving as museum teacher at the Los Angeles Children's Museum. She has published and presented on cross-cultural perspectives on play and learning in the United States and Denmark. She received her PhD in Social and Philosophical Foundations in Education, Educational Administration, and Anthropology from Cornell University.

Laura Bigaouette is Assistant Dean for Outreach in Manhattanville's School of Education. In this capacity, she serves as Director of the CSI and School of Education Alumni Relations. She initiated the parent-education component of CSI because of her involvement with the Hispanic community and, as a result, developed the annual Hispanic Parents Leadership Institute to help parents learn about the U.S. educational system. She also runs all events related to CSI, including the consortium and the annual conference. Laura has over fifteen years of experience in corporate marketing management, international marketing, and consulting. As a Senior Consultant at Telcordia Technologies, Laura worked with international client companies in Egypt, Mexico, and Ecuador on strategic and tactical market solutions. She has experience in creating and implementing strategic marketing plans, business plans, and tactics to advance a business's competitive positioning. As the marketing project director at Verizon International, Laura worked extensively on branding, communications strategies, market research, and competitive analysis on projects in Asia and Europe with significant project experience in Thailand, Indonesia, Taiwan, and the Philippines. Laura is the President and Founder of New View Coaching and is a certified life coach. Since 2003, she has worked with individuals, nonprofits, and business organizations on marketing, leadership, and personal coaching. Laura has an MBA in International Marketing from Pace University.

Part 1

The Challenges of Changing Suburban School Districts

1

The Changing Suburbs

Imagine this situation. In a suburban Midwestern town lives a white, middle-class family, the Martins, where the father is a manager of a local department store and the mother is a housewife. They have three daughters, ages seven through fourteen. Each night, when the father comes home, he looks forward to his wife's home-cooked meal and his daughters' stories about their day. He helps his daughters with any homework that has not already been completed and works with his wife to prepare his daughters for bedtime. The mother is very active in the PTA at both the elementary and middle schools and does everything to help their three daughters with school and their extracurricular activities. The family owns and lives in a single-family home in a quiet and spacious suburban neighborhood where all the other white families have children about the same age. The families depend on each other for carpooling, babysitting, and emergency situations and attend social events at each other's homes. As with the other families in the neighborhood, the Martins are very pleased with their predominantly white local schools and cannot imagine living anywhere else as they raise their children.

T his situation portrays suburban life in general decades ago. The image of living in the suburbs meant that the husband, wife, and children lived in a comfortable home in a homogeneous community of like-minded people. The suburbs were considered a place to raise children while avoiding having to brush shoulders with the poor (Miller, 1995; Press, 2007). Such an image began to fade when increasing numbers of minorities moved to the suburbs, creating sociological, economic, and educational changes.

This first chapter forms the basis for the rest of the book by discussing the concept and demographics of the changing suburbs and the impact of such changes on schools. Characteristics of changing suburban schools are described as a backdrop for a general set of ideas and guidelines for school leaders.

What Do We Mean by the Changing Suburbs?

To understand the changing suburbs, we first need to know about the suburbs in general. A suburban area is a residential community adjacent to or within commuting distance of a city that has a lower population density than a city. The Department of Justice defines a suburban area as a Census Block Group no more than thirty miles from an urban area or a Census Block Group with a density greater than or equal to 500 people per square mile and less than 2,000 people per square mile (U.S. Department of Justice, 2008). Generally speaking, the suburbs refer to housing developments and neighborhoods within commuting distance of large cities where crime is low, schools are good, few people are poor, and nearly everyone is white (Bell & Newby, 1974).

The phenomenon of the changing suburbs in the United States refers to a mix of people of all races and ethnicities, low-income families, and apartment dwellers that has occurred in suburbs during the last few decades (Harris, 1999; Miller, 1995) as a result of migration patterns from urban areas and immigration patterns from other countries. As reported in a *Newsweek* magazine article (January 17, 2009), the suburbs are no longer just middle-class families expressed in stucco and brick but rather resemble noisy, diverse, striving, and poor cities. Although changes to suburbs surrounding large cities such as Los Angeles, Chicago, Washington, DC, Houston, and New York have been particularly acute because of high minority populations (Evans, 2007), changes in the suburbs are occurring throughout the country.

These rapidly changing suburbs are beginning to create hurdles very similar to those faced by cities where there are failed businesses, neighborhoods of increasing poverty, and new challenges for schools. A senior research analyst at the Brookings Institution's Metropolitan Policy Program said that American poverty has become increasingly suburban. Major metropolitan suburban areas have seen their poor populations increase by 25 percent over the last decade, which is the largest and fastest-growing poverty demographic area in the country (Yaccino, 2010).

Evolution of the Middle-Class Suburbs

Prior to the Civil War, some of the earliest suburbs were developed to provide housing for those too poor to afford the protection of city walls. After the Civil War, the suburbs became a place for the wealthy to separate work from home and redefine family as a unit focused on raising children rather than as a center for economic activity. Wealthy urbanites built homes in the suburbs to escape the congestion, disease, and unrest of city life. After World War II, suburbs became havens for whites in general who fled their urban enclaves that had become crowded, dirty, and populated by poor and immigrant families. Migration to the suburbs was largely motivated by a desire to escape the mix of classes and racial or ethnic groups that characterized urban areas. The middle class had the same desire as the wealthy to have a graceful home life away from the *riffraff* of the city (Garnett, 2007; Miller, 1995). The middle class found that they could be employed in different industries in the suburbs because of developments in both technology and the highway system (University of Cincinnati, 2010). Although there was never a time when all suburbs were a safe and wonderful means of escape, the gap between real and imagined U.S. suburbs has widened.

Immigration and Its Impact on the Suburbs

When immigrants first entered the United States, they first resided in the cities and then, after many generations, moved to the suburbs. Today, suburban settlements are emerging as a hallmark of contemporary immigration to the United States, particularly for the Asian and Hispanic populations (Fessenden, 2007). Not only are immigrants moving directly to the suburbs, but they also are moving from urban ethnic enclaves to take advantage of the schools, economic opportunities, and the feeling of safety. They are achieving favorable neighborhood amenities without undergoing assimilation

(Alba, Logan, Stults, Marzan, & Zhang, 1999); in other words, they are moving from urban enclaves to suburban communities where their ethnic majority predominates.

These suburban enclaves are mimicking urban enclaves, with reports of downward mobility for some immigrant populations. For instance, day laborers gather every morning on street corners or in parking lots, hoping to get work, which is at best seasonal and sporadic. They usually do not have medical coverage for their injuries from their day jobs and often live in poverty and with poor health. High unemployment has resulted in more people requesting social services such as emergency food and housing relief, job training, and help with health care. Yet, even with these problems and needs, immigrants want their children to grow up in the suburbs rather than on city streets strewn with crack vials and gang graffiti (Press, 2007).

Social services, usually a focus for urban areas, now must be part of policymakers' agendas so that funds are made available to immigrants and others living in poverty (Yaccino, 2010).

Patterns of Change

Social scientists have been studying the different patterns of migration within the suburbs. In-group attraction and out-group avoidance has emerged as one idea for explaining the furthering of boundaries between ethnic groups. The principle of homophily, or being attracted to those like oneself and being repelled by others who are racially different, explains why different races move to areas that already have a sizable number of the same race. For example, African Americans often move into areas that already have a sizable number of African Americans or other racial minorities. Whites often leave areas where African Americans or other racial minorities are an everlarger majority. There also is the concept of spatial assimilation where upwardly mobile minorities prefer to move to suburban areas that are predominantly white to help them become more fully integrated (Hwang & Murdock, 1998; Richard, 2000).

As minorities move into different suburban areas, white flight becomes more prominent, leading to suburban sprawl or increases in developed land without population increases (Vandegrift & Yoked, 2004). White suburbanites move from one suburb to another because of racism, economic calculation, the hope for a community of like-minded people, and the attempt to find an environment good for family life (Miller, 1995). Some social scientists refer to this migration as moving from inner-ring suburbs, which contain more diversity, to outer-ring suburbs (University of Cincinnati, 2010). Such migration is more appealing to white and Asian populations, who do not want to be in crowded suburban areas, than to African American and Hispanic populations, who are not as affected by density (Garnett, 2007).

Social scientists have concluded that not all suburbs are the same. The degree of poverty and the number and type of immigrant and minority populations vary from suburb to suburb. One suburban community can be mostly affluent while a nearby community can have a high concentration of poor people. Another suburban community can have an affluent side of town and an impoverished side of town where the people from the impoverished side clean homes, mow lawns, staff restaurants, and clean offices for the affluent populations. Some suburban areas continue to be affluent and increasingly diverse as African American families and other minority groups experience rising incomes. Suburbs also are characterized by different minority groups. In the New York area there are sizable Hispanic populations in the suburbs, while in the Washington, DC, area there are substantial African American and Asian populations in the suburbs (Press, 2007; University of Chicago, 2010).

Schools in the Changing Suburbs

Suburban schools are a major attraction to minority populations because of their reputation for providing significantly better educational opportunities than their urban counterparts. Many suburban schools have gone from serving predominantly white students to serving mostly minority students. West Windsor-Plainsboro Regional School District in New Jersey exemplifies this shift from serving an all-white population to serving a one-third minority population. As with other changing suburban school districts, the growth changed the social dynamics in the schools and in the community. Parents complained about opportunities being "taken away" from their children by newcomers. Incidents of violence with racial overtones ensued, and many parents feared for their children's safety. African American students complained that they were punished more severely than white students committing the same offenses, while white students believed that African American students were getting away with everything because the teachers were afraid to deal with them (Badlow, 2001).

With this relatively new phenomenon of having minority students in suburban schools, racial beliefs and assumptions are tested with interactions between teachers, students, and administrators. Allocation of resources (knowledge, power, human, and financial) has become an issue with respect to the interests of minority students (Evans, 2007). Power and political struggles have emerged as administrators, teachers, and the community figure out ways to balance personal and organizational needs and interests. Suburban schools are indeed changing to the point of needing to be redefined to accommodate the changing student population that is often characterized by low student achievement, mobility, poverty, and language differences.

Although changing suburban schools are beginning to have many of the characteristics of urban schools, they nevertheless are different. They do in fact have resources to deploy that come from their local communities. They do not have the level of violence, often spawned by gangs, that urban schools have. They have their own local school boards that work in concert with school administrators and the community to make decisions about school expenditures and polices. Historically, white suburban schools are in a sense experiencing their unique coming-of-age stories as they grapple with the changing faces that now occupy their classrooms.

Many of these changing faces come from Spanish-speaking countries. Because such immigrants are very diverse in their national origins, ethnic, religious, and class backgrounds, they require increased attention from school leaders and their teachers (Denton, Hernandez, & Macartney, 2009). Unfortunately, collecting accurate data about these immigrant children may not be a priority for schools because they assume that immigrants:

- lack a strong or vocal political base from which to advocate for their needs
- have language barriers that interfere with school-family communication
- do not understand their rights as parents, feel comfortable discussing their concerns with educators, or comprehend U.S. schooling practices
- have limited educational attainment, live in poverty, and suffer difficulties such as unstable employment and overcrowded housing

Assumptions, however, cannot be made about newly arrived immigrant students and their prior experience in school. Many immigrant children are well educated, while others are minimally educated, depending on school attendance opportunities prior to entry into the United States. Some come from sound educational infrastructures from their home countries, whereas others have interrupted schooling because of poverty, civil strife, and war (Goodwin, 2002). Voluntary immigrants have an easier time integrating into the United States than those uprooted from their countries because of persecution and fear of death. Nevertheless, the educational success of this rapidly growing immigrant children population merits increased attention from school administrators, teachers, and public officials.

Facing the Challenges of Changing Suburban Schools

There are many competing forces in changing suburban schools. On the one hand is the existing organizational culture that makes change efforts difficult and complex; on the other hand is the urgent need to change the culture to accommodate a different type of student learner. Everyone involved is struggling to address these competing forces so that students are acculturated into the schools. Native-born minorities usually differ in socioeconomic status from native-born majorities, whereas immigrant children usually differ in the area of language. Support for these different types of learners needs to vary in order to address students' needs.

School leaders must take the lead in adjusting to the changes so that they can help their teaching staff face the challenges that surround them. Teachers need to become adept at developing multiple ways of tapping into students' funds of knowledge as a scaffold for new learning (Goodwin, 2002). Before teachers develop new ways of teaching, they need to become open minded and well prepared to work with students who are different from them. Teachers' resistance to change is one of the more difficult challenges to overcome because parochial attitudes toward diverse student populations can negatively impact student achievement. Students need to change as well so that they are less prejudiced toward others who are different from them.

West Windsor-Plainsboro Regional School District mentioned above made great strides in changing the course of race relations. The superintendent created a task force on bigotry that included the high school principal, parents, students, and teachers and focused on building positive human relations and mutual respect among students and faculty. The task force implemented a new student code of conduct with highly prescriptive regulations that gave administrators little latitude in assigning penalties. The greatest return on prejudice reduction may have come from insisting that students take more responsibility for their own behavior and that of others. The effort began by engaging students in age-appropriate awareness programs on topics such as racism, the Holocaust, gender bias, sexual harassment, substance abuse, and homophobia (Badlow, 2001).

As noted in the preface, the Changing Suburbs Institute has professional development schools (PDS) that have taken different routes to help address increases in their Hispanic populations. One school led the way in becoming a community school so that the school could provide before- and after-school services to its mostly immigrant population: parenting workshops, social work, and medical and dental appointments. Community school services helped the parents feel more empowered to work with the schools. See Chapter 7 for a full description.

Three PDS schools implemented dual language programs to help students learn two languages, English and Spanish, at once. Dual language programs develop academic literacy in English and another language simultaneously. English learners and English proficient learners share the same dual language classroom setting. Longitudinal research on this model has indicated enhanced student outcomes for second language learners (Collier & Thomas, 2004). See Chapter 5 for more information.

One school brought in Sheltered Instruction Observation Protocol (SIOP), focused on data-driven lesson plans to make content comprehensible. One school adopted the international baccalaureate as a collaborative teaching framework for teaching and learning that is founded on student inquiry, internationalism, and building character. Two schools implemented professional learning communities to provide teachers with common collaboration time to support children's success.

All eight of these PDSs have principals who are acutely aware of the demographic changes in their schools and are actively involved with their administrative and teaching staff to identify effective strategies to accommodate student needs. These principals also have as a priority the ongoing professional development of their teachers. They work with us as a local college to provide additional resources and work closely with their respective communities to garner support for their teachers.

School leaders are the key to bringing about needed changes. The following four guidelines are offered to help school leaders get a head start in moving forward to bring together the community on behalf of its students.

- Study demographics
- Form networks
- Learn about programs
- Create a culture of acceptance

Guidelines for Moving Forward

Study Demographics

In order to be able to manage change, one needs to know what the change is. As Evans (2007) discovered when she worked with three different schools, changing demographics redefines schools or gives them an uncertain identity. Our work with the Changing Suburbs Institute professional development schools has shown that, while all eight schools have had an increase of 7 percent or more in Hispanic students in the last four years, they still are very different demographically and, as a result, have very different needs. Six schools have Hispanic students as the majority student population (ranging from 45 percent to 93 percent), one school has white students as the majority (70 percent), and one school has African American students as the majority (49 percent). Four schools are primarily Hispanic and African American, whereas the other four are primarily Hispanic and white, with either Hispanic students or white students in the majority. These demographics provide different portraits of student needs, especially in relation to standardized testing, dropout and graduation rates, and college acceptance rates.

Guidelines for Moving Forward

- Study demographics
- Form networks
- Learn about programs
- Create a culture of acceptance

The predominantly white district continues to be able to highlight its merit scholars, Ivy League college acceptance rates, and advanced placement test scores. The predominantly Hispanic and Hispanic/African American schools are focused on statewide standardized tests pass rates and possibly two-year and four-year college acceptance rates. Understanding the demographics is crucial for setting realistic goals for the school and district.

Demographics, or the attributes of a population in a particular geographical area, usually include race, ethnic origin, income, age range, gender, occupation, employment status, education, family size, religion, spoken language, disabilities, mobility, and home ownership. Demographic trends describe the changes in demographics in a population over time (for example, the average age of a population may increase or decrease over time). The National Center for Education Statistics (NCES) of the United States Department of Education looks at information about demographics, which includes social and economic characteristics of children and school districts. These pieces of information all influence students. Demographics show that students living in poverty struggle more in school than those coming from middle-class families. Statistically, parents who read to their children on a regular basis are married, educated, and employed (Moss, n.d.).

Effective superintendents know that they need to

- study the demographic trends in their districts to understand school capacity, zoning, and future growth;
- bring in demographers and financial teams to help study the demographic trends; and
- use written surveys, town hall meetings, and focus groups to gather feedback from the community to be able to develop realistic goals (Gentle, 2011; Lindsey, 2011).

Demographic trend data enable superintendents and their administrative teams to address current educational and financial needs and plan for future changes so that schools have the necessary resources for working with the changing student population. For example, one of the PDSs described above went from serving primarily African American students to serving both Hispanic and African American students. Because demographic trend data indicated that an increasing number of immigrants were moving into this district, the superintendent and principal worked feverishly to investigate and eventually open a Newcomer Center for immigrants to help them become properly enrolled and engaged in the district.

Form Networks

A silver bullet does not exist to help low achievers transform into high achievers. Educators need other educators to help them puzzle their way through their unique situations to address student achievement challenges. Recently, national and regional networks have been formed with suburban school district leaders to enable them to work with each other to improve the educational experiences and outcomes of all students, with a particular focus on minority students. One of the first groups to form is the national Minority Student Achievement Network, which is a coalition of twenty-five multiracial suburban-urban districts with a history of high achievement that work together to examine practices that affect the academic performance of students from diverse backgrounds. Bedford Central School District in Westchester, New York, has been a member of the Minority Student Achievement Network since 2004 because of its ability to network with other districts that are experiencing similar demographic changes. See Superintendent Jere Hochman's thoughts in Box 1.1.

Box 1.1 From the Superintendent's Desk on Forming Networks

Superintendent Jere Hochman has the opportunity to communicate with others who are trying to address similar challenges. He also is able to involve his staff in conducting and sharing research with other members of the network. The network validates what his district already is doing and, at the same time, exposes him to what other districts are doing that could possibly work in his district. While the network serves an important purpose in sharing best practices and acquiring resources through grants to try new ideas, Jere acknowledges that because the districts are not local, it is sometimes difficult for him and his staff to travel to the conferences that are offered through the network. The idea of being physically together to exchange ideas is one of the benefits of regional networks. (J. Hochman, personal communication, August 8, 2011)

Regional groups such as the Delaware Valley Student Achievement Consortium and the New Jersey Network were spawned from the national Minority Student Achievement Network to bring together school leaders. There also was a group developed through the National Staff Development Council to connect twelve schools to raise student achievement in under twelve years. Called *12 under 12*, this group is in response to the No Child Left Behind Act. See Figure 1.1 for a description of each of these networks.

The Changing Suburbs Institute has collaborated with the Penn Center for Educational Leadership at the University of Pennsylvania and Putnam/Northern Westchester Board of Cooperative Educational Services (BOCES) Center for Educational Leadership to develop the Lower Hudson Valley Consortium for Excellence and Equity. This network was modeled after the regional consortia in Delaware Valley and New Jersey. School district superintendents in the Lower Hudson Valley Region of New York volunteered to pay a fee to work with other superintendents to develop systemwide approaches for improving the academic performance of all students and eliminating the observed achievement disparities among subgroups of students defined by race, ethnicity, or economic circumstance. Member districts

- received professional development from nationally recognized scholars and practitioners on creative and innovative strategies for addressing student achievement,
- identified ways to improve students' language and literacy,

Figure 1.1 Networks to Close the Achievement Gap in Changing Suburban School Districts

Network Name	Description	General Information	Website Address
Minority Student Achievement Network (MSAN)	A national coalition of 25 multiracial, suburban–urban school districts that study and eliminate the achievement gaps that exist in their districts.	Begun in 1999, MSAN has worked to achieve the parallel goals of closing achievement gaps that persist in their districts while ensuring all students achieve to high levels. Districts, which share a history of high achievement, work collaboratively to conduct and publish research, analyze policies, and examine practices that affect the academic performance of students from diverse backgrounds, specifically African American and Latino/Latina students.	http://msan.wceruw.org/
Delaware Valley Student Achievement Consortium	A collaborative association of 28 regional school districts and four county intermediate units in the greater Philadelphia region committed to working together to enhance the achievement and well-being of all of their students by reducing the disparities in achievement and school engagement between African American and Hispanic students and their Caucasian and Asian peers.	Begun in 2004, the Delaware Valley Student Achievement Consortium has worked to improve the educational experiences and outcomes of all students in districts across Pennsylvania, New Jersey, and Delaware. It serves as a resource for school district superintendents and their leadership teams to refine policies and practices to close the achievement gap. It provides professional learning experiences for students, teachers, counselors, principals, central office administrators, and school boards. It is a program of the Penn Center for Educational Leadership of the Graduate School of Education of the University of Pennsylvania.	http://www.gse.upenn.edu/pcel/programs/dvmsac

New Jersey Network	A regional network of school districts in New Jersey committed to actively reducing the gaps in achievement and school engagement among disaggregated populations, African American, Latino/Latina, gender issues, and special needs students.	Begun in 2007, the Educational Information and Resource Center (EIRC) and the Penn Center for Educational Leadership at the University of Pennsylvania collaborated to: • acknowledge and explore the root causes of their achievement gaps; • actively collaborate with other network districts to measurably close the gaps; • actively change school structures, policies, and practices; • develop annual district plans for closing the gaps; • share promising professional practices with one another.	http://www.eirc.org/website/teacher-resources/nj-network-to-close-the-achievement-gap/
The National Staff Development Council (NSDC)—*12 Under 12* Network	The NSDC involves twelve schools committed to raising performance for ALL students in under twelve years. The schools participate in a network called *12 under 12*, which provides high-quality staff development, in combination with other reforms, to help all students become academically proficient.	The National Staff Development Council formed this group in 2003 to prod schools to move more quickly than the federal government's requirement that every student meet or exceed proficiency on statewide assessments in math and language arts before 2014. Among other benefits, districts have an annual site visit from a NSDC staff person and monthly conference calls with other network members. Network members include schools across the United States with different enrollment sizes, different grade levels, and different community types.	http://www.learningforward.org/about/12under12.cfm

- discussed ideas for building caring school and classroom cultures with high expectations, and
- shared promising systemic strategies that have proven to be successful in addressing achievement needs of minority student populations.

These school district superintendents have come to appreciate that, while they have their own unique combinations of student, teacher, parent, and community challenges, they also share common concerns when it comes to curriculum, instruction, and assessment practices that need to be adjusted. They have determined that it is useful for them to become part of a network that can communicate and collaborate on ways to improve their schools.

Learn About Programs

Knowledge of a district's current and future demographics, combined with opportunities to network with others, will contribute to an understanding of the best types of programs that should and can be implemented in a district. Successfully seeking a school board's financial support for additional programs and personnel depends on the community's understanding of the changing demographics in the district and the impact that these changes are having on students' academic performance which in turn affects a district's property values and overall reputation. Support also depends on an appreciation of the types of educational opportunities that are needed to stem any downward trends.

School superintendents need to help their school boards understand what is realistic and what is not, given the nature of the changing student population. As Karen List said about her suburban school district's growing achievement gap, "It's certainly much more than what we can do in a school district. It's housing, it's pre-K, it's prenatal" (Butrymowicz, 2011, para. 26). Yet, much still can be done to help both students and their parents. Promising practices have been studied for helping minority and immigrant students. Such practices include pre-K in public schools; after-school tutoring programs; parent outreach and training; newcomer and family resource centers; school-based community centers; different types of specialists to assist teachers in literacy, special education, and English as a second language (ESL); social workers to help families with everyday living challenges; ESL pullout programs; teen pregnancy prevention programs; and dual language programs. Figure 1.2 provides examples of

Figure 1.2 Examples of Instructional Programs in Changing Suburban School Districts

Type of District or School	Program	Description	Source
Large suburban school district in the Midwest	Dual language Spanish–English program	• Piloted K–6 dual language in one elementary school. • Expanding to include 29 other elementary schools with a focus on teaching English and Spanish simultaneously to children whose first language can be either. • Will offer one-way dual language, which focuses on Spanish-speaking English learners, and two-way dual language, which focuses on students who are dominant in either English or Spanish. Program begins in kindergarten with 80% of time in Spanish and 20% in English; will go to 50% in Spanish and 50% in English by third grade (Bruno, 2010).	http://www.mysuburbanlife.com/ itasca/newsnow/ x829118432/U-46-to-expand-dual -language-program
Suburban elementary school in an affluent suburban district in the Northeast	• Evening programs for parents • Hired new Spanish speaking teachers • Hired new literacy coaches • Decreased class size • Hired full-time reading specialist • Hired full-time social worker • Hired additional teachers at one elementary school who speak Spanish • Hired a literacy coach for teachers • Hired a full-time social worker and converted the reading specialist position to full time	• The principal initiated evening programs in Spanish and urged parents to attend. • Reduced class size in K–2 to 15, while kept at 22 for the three other elementary schools. • Computer laboratories were kept, even though cut at the other elementary schools (Fessenden, 2007).	http://www.nytimes.com/2007/12/16/ nyregion/ nyregionspecial2/16Rschool.html?pa gewanted=1&ref=bilingualeducation

(Continued)

Figure 1.2 *(Continued)*

Type of District or School	Program	Description	Source
Large suburban school district in the Midwest with growing English language learners (ELL) population across the district	• Family welcome center for immigrants • ESL program • Sheltered Instruction Observation Protocol (SIOP)	• Intake specialist assesses student's language and math proficiency and makes academic recommendations; assists with all facets of the registration process for school, including free and reduced lunch and transportation. • Provides ESL program to students who qualify due to a family language other than English combined with test scores that show lack of proficiency in English; licensed ESL teachers provide direct instruction in English and the use of English in other content areas; paraeducators also support classroom instruction in some schools; instruction takes place in mainstream classrooms and pullout setting. • Uses eight features of SIOP model in the mainstream classroom to help make content comprehensible: preparation, building background, comprehensible input, strategies, interaction, practice and application, lesson delivery, and review and assessment.	http://www.anoka.k12.mn.us/ education/components/faq/faq.php? sectiondetailid=232590&#answer_1

| Suburban elementary school in the Northeast with growing immigrant population across the district | Full-service community school | • Created a community school to provide community health and social services to students and their families.
• Provides extended learning opportunities for enrichment and remediation through the school's after-school and summer programs.
• Improved academic programs through targeted professional development and teacher induction to improve teacher quality through onsite school–university partnerships (Martin, Fergus, & Noguera, 2010). | http://www.eric.ed.gov/ ERICWebPortal/search/detailmini. jsp?_nfpb=true&_&ERICExtSearch_ SearchValue_0=EJ886100&ERICExt Search_ SearchType_0=no&accno=EJ886100 |
| Large suburban school district in the Northeast with growing ELL population | • SIOP
• Classroom-based professional development | • Provides a comprehensive lesson planning and delivery system.
• Works with graduate education faculty to come into their classrooms to serve as their eyes and ears about teacher's instructional practices, facilitate team meetings, and co-teach; helps teachers use cooperating learning techniques, more visuals and graphic organizers, additional materials with bilingual glossaries, and structured, scaffolded explanations of directions or assignments (Giouroukakis, Cohan, Nenchin, & Honigsfeld, 2011). | http://www.learningforward.org/ news/getDocument. cfm?articleID=2293 |

successful programs and initiatives adopted by suburban schools and school districts. Chapter 5 provides more information about many of these programs.

Create a Culture of Acceptance

Creating a culture of acceptance means that teachers, staff, and administrators celebrate the diversity in a school and district. See Principal Annemarie Berardi's thoughts in Box 1.2. They monitor their own behavior in responding to students so that they are not interacting differently with students of different races or high and low achievers. Teachers are aware of their course content and material so that it is free of stereotypes, reevaluate their own pedagogical methods for teaching diverse students, help students avoid racist and

Box 1.2 From the Principal's Desk on Creating a Culture of Acceptance

Annemarie Berardi, principal of Fox Lane Middle School in Bedford School District, New York, believes that a hallmark of her school and her district is the culture of acceptance that she and her administrative and teaching staff have created over time for all students. Before her students even arrive from their elementary schools, which are clearly different in both socioeconomic status and levels of diversity, she and her staff bring the students and parents together so that they begin to see themselves as one middle school community. She and her staff have created school-wide lessons on acceptance where they discuss the importance of respecting others, in spite of differences in race, ethnic background, and social class. Her middle school teachers know that their job is to learn about each student (for example, articulating with previous teachers and taking social histories) to help each learn as best as possible. Although she knows that there continue to be gaps in achievement, she also knows that she and her staff have made great strides in being able to anticipate and address student-learning issues by staying on message about the importance of honoring and educating all students. She is particularly proud of the schoolwide lessons that have been created to communicate to students that disrespect and bullying will not be tolerated. She also is aware that every effort to modify the curriculum and improve instruction is a work in progress. Yet she and her staff are determined that students will not "fall through the cracks, no matter what!" (A. Berardi, personal communication, July 15, 2011) other types of discriminatory remarks on school grounds, and aim for inclusion with all class assignments (Davis, 2009).

Superintendents and principals are essential for setting the tone for cultural acceptance through their words and actions. Such acceptance needs to be extended to the parents and community. The benefits of such leadership and outreach are reflected in the administrator and teacher teamwork at Annandale High School, a diverse suburban school outside Washington, DC, which determined that any effort to become a model diverse school had to involve the parents from all cultures. The team realized that translating flyers for current programs into Spanish and other languages or inviting parents to Back-to-School Night without explanation did not bring parents to the school because these materials and messages lacked meaning to immigrant parents. With the help of a grant for an Immigrant Parent Leadership Initiative, the school was able to offer parent-leader classes in English and Spanish to empower parents to become leaders in their own families, schools, and communities; offer programs for parents from specific ethnic groups in Spanish, Korean, and Vietnamese; guide teachers in action research to increase their understanding of parents from other cultures; and open a parent resource center. Immigrant parents now are taking leadership roles in the school and, because of better connections with immigrant parents, teachers are reporting improvement in students' academic achievement (Sobel & Kugler, 2007). There is no one way to develop a culture of acceptance with students and their parents, but it truly is a first step in communicating to an increasingly diverse student and parent population that they are valued members of a school district community.

Concluding Remarks

The suburbs no longer simply resemble the homogeneity portrayed in the opening vignette. Instead, and throughout the country, the suburbs resemble multiracial and multicultural cities that have pockets of poverty, overcrowded housing, and crime. The schools, as a reflection of the changing suburban population, must accept and address the needs of their changing student populations with newfound attitudes, programs, and instructional methodologies. These suburban schools now have some of the same challenges that impoverished urban and rural schools have had and need to seek assistance in providing the necessary social and educational services to help with student achievement. School leaders, as key spokespersons and role models for their schools and districts, have the responsibility of ensuring that *all* students are given every opportunity to learn in an accepting, supportive, and culturally relevant atmosphere. School leaders who are open minded, self-reflective, collaborative, strategic, and determined will be able to ensure that their administrative and teaching staff is equipped to be successful with their students, their parents, and the community.

2

The School Leader's Role in the Changing Suburbs

The story of Blytheville, a suburban district in central Texas, illustrates the importance of school leaders when school districts change. The superintendent and school board ran the district with full parental support for the status quo of this farming community. The population changed in two distinctly different ways. Young white professionals with children moved into one area, demanding college-preparatory courses and gifted and talented programs. Primarily Spanish-speaking Hispanic parents moved into another area with mobile homes and brought with them challenges of high unemployment, substandard living, and low socioeconomic status. This fast-growing group of children was characterized as highly mobile and at risk for failure. Blytheville now had three distinct communities of children attending the schools.

While the superintendent tried to adjust to overcrowding, sociological changes, and school board changes, he eventually was forced to resign because of others' perceptions that he held on to outdated concepts of school administration. His successors did not do much better. Within seven years, the district had five new superintendents and three new principals because of the struggles between administrators and board members who interfered with the day-to-day management of the school district.

Eventually, enough members of the school board changed for them to realize that they needed to reach out to the state for help, which included a designated master to take complete control of the district. This experienced child-centered interim administrator, with strong knowledge of school finance, school law, and administrative practices, helped the school board develop a shared vision that encompassed the changing community. He also reached out to civic groups and local churches to be involved in the schools and brought the community together so that it could coexist with a new superintendent. When another new superintendent finally came to the district, he came with his eyes wide open about the years of strife and many divisions within the community. He knew that he needed to get support for a shared vision of learning for all students and collaborate with families and community members to mobilize resources for the district's diverse needs and interests.

Source: From "The Blytheville Story: The Challenge of Changing Demographics," by S. Lowery and S. Harris, 2002, *Journal of Cases in Educational Leadership, 5*(3), 49–55. Reprinted with permission.

With changing demographics and growing diversity in communities, school leaders must first have a clear understanding of a community so that the schools can mirror the communities surrounding it. Effective leaders understand that their tenure in an administrative position is largely influenced by the community and the attitudes of the teachers, the school board, and the administration. They know how to collaborate with their diverse communities so that they are bound by a shared ideology, which in turn is shared and implemented by school district employees.

This chapter discusses the roles and responsibilities of superintendents and principals in adjusting to changes in suburban school districts. To understand some of the unique aspects of such a leadership role, it is important to take a step back to look at role similarities and differences for such administrators in both urban and rural districts.

Role Similarities and Differences for Urban, Rural, and Suburban Leaders

Urban Leaders

Urban school superintendents are responsible for large bureaucratic districts that have complex internal and external politics and pressures from the schools, communities, school board, and city government. Urban superintendents are challenged by intensifying levels of poverty, the changing conditions of families, declining resources, an increasing number of children in poor health, limited English proficiency of students and their families, low achievement among minority students, and escalating violence and crime in and around the schools. Urban superintendents must constantly fight for the financial lives of their districts so that they have the resources needed to help their students learn. This fight is especially intense with the burgeoning array of charter schools and magnet schools that compete for the same funds and usually take the top students. With pressure to raise student achievement in an arena of impossible odds for success there is a high rate of turnover among urban superintendents' (Wimpelberg, 1997).

Urban principals are part of similarly large bureaucratic structures with high per pupil expenditure, minimal local revenue, and high percentages of students at risk for school failure. Urban principals must search for resources for their schools and often use their schools as centers for needed social, medical, psychological, and educational services.

Urban principals are confronted with teachers' sense of hopelessness because of gaps in students' experiential learning, violent behavior, lack of motivation, and parent apathy. An inexperienced teaching force, lack of decision-making authority, lack of parent involvement, high dropout rate, lack of funding, and loss of students to other schools lead to a high turnover rate among urban principals (Erwin, Winn, Gentry, & Cauble, 2010; Portin, 2000).

One of our colleagues, who actually thrived as an urban principal in New York City, is more concerned than ever about principals being expected to do more with less. He talks about the disconnect between what is mandated by federal, state, and city government and what is realistic in the time allocated. He worries about teachers' morale and hopes that public officials will continue to focus on improving the communities in which these students reside.

Rural Leaders

Rural superintendents are responsible for districts that are geographically isolated. They often preside over districts that are racially similar, have below-standard educational outcomes (only two-thirds might graduate from high school), and have fairly high poverty levels. Depending on the geographic location, there are declining enrollments that affect the level of state funding and, in turn, the need to consolidate schools (Browne-Ferrigno & Allen, 2006; Loveland, 2002).

With fewer students and staff, rural superintendents usually are paid less yet are asked to assume a greater number of responsibilities.

For example, a superintendent might also be the director of curriculum and business manager. Community scrutiny and resistance can create difficulties for rural superintendents who stray from the norm on the way things are expected to be done. Financial shortfalls often limit the types of educational services (special education classrooms, advanced placement courses, and foreign language programs) that superintendents can provide and require them to share services with other districts. They often have trouble recruiting teachers from outside the district because of the district's location and the low teacher salaries. As with urban superintendents, rural superintendents' attrition rates are high (Erwin et al., 2010).

Rural principals also are paid less and asked to do more. A colleague shared that when she thought that she was being hired to be the principal of an elementary school in a small town in North Carolina, she discovered that she was to be the principal for the elementary school *and* the middle school. This meant that she was responsible for two schools at two different levels, with more than double the paperwork. After many attempts to try to manage the many layers of responsibility without any administrative assistance, she determined that she needed to search for a different type of district.

Rural principals do have fewer students and have teachers who report satisfaction with their teaching conditions. They also have teachers who report dissatisfaction because their students have limited aspirations, stemming mostly from parents' lack of understanding of the importance of an education for the future. Some rural principals and their teachers are encountering dramatic and often confusing changes with the in-migration of well-educated telecommuters who are asking for a reassessment of their schools' goals (Howley, Howley, & Larson, 1999). Elementary principal Donald Buckingham explains that in his elementary school, which is located in a small coastal town in Sedgwick, Maine, half of his children are eligible for free and reduced lunch and the other half are not because they come from affluent families (Loveland, 2002). Turnover rate is high among rural principals because the schools are generally seen as inferior and deficient (Budge, 2006; Erwin et al., 2010; Howley et al., 1999).

Suburban Leaders

Suburban superintendents are usually associated with school districts in neighborhoods with educated, two-parent families and low rates of poverty. Resources from both schools and families make it easier to educate students, allowing for high pass rates on standardized tests, low dropout rates, and high college acceptance rates. The life span of suburban superintendents is usually longer than that of other district administrators because they are able to be effective both fiscally and instructionally. While a significant amount of their time requires their responsiveness to parent interest and expectations, their message of high-quality instruction as a priority helps them politically with their parent constituency (Daresh & Aplin, 2001; Erwin et al., 2010; Roscigno, Tomaskovic-Devey, & Crowley, 2006).

Suburban principals have been easy to recruit and retain for many of the same reasons as suburban superintendents. Suburban principals in turn have had their pick of teachers because of their desire to teach in suburban schools. Funds have been readily available for offering programs to accommodate differing student needs, and parents have worked alongside their suburban principals to help with resources and services. For example, an elementary principal was able to hire a math teacher and a reading teacher for the sole purpose of pulling out his advanced students at all grade levels for accelerated math and reading instruction; a middle school principal was able to hire a teacher to teach Chinese and a teacher to teach Farsi for the foreign language block; and a high school principal was able to develop a theater education program that funded local actors and dancers who would mentor students on a daily basis for the school's highly celebrated productions.

However, many 21st century suburban superintendents and principals do not have the kind of discretionary funds that they had in the past. Marc Bernstein, superintendent of Valley Stream Central High School District in Long Island, New York, has attested to this change. When he first arrived on Long Island as assistant superintendent in 1977, practically all of his students were white and spoke English as their primary language. Today, Long Island's suburban school districts have experienced a growth of 7 to 14 percentage points in their minority student populations because of the arrival of immigrants and the migration of minorities from New York City.

He and his colleague superintendents are experiencing increased violence and gangs at the schoolhouse doors and are forced to choose between providing security or needed instructional programs for their changing student population. One school district has even been taken over by the state because of its academic and financial struggles. As Marc Bernstein explains, funds are needed to support special programs for students and parents, and professional development programs are needed to help teachers learn new instructional strategies for working with a different student population. At the very least, he wishes that there were government support and different funding options that recognize these demographic shifts (Bernstein, 2004).

With demographic shifts in suburban neighborhoods, school leaders are urged to be resourceful in building the capacity of their schools, even as these schools face financial issues and have predominantly white faculties who often have deficit views about minority students' learning abilities (Erwin et al., 2010).

Challenges for School Leaders in Changing Suburban School Districts

Superintendents set the tone and direction for the district. As both internal and external leaders, they look to their administrative teams to steer and oversee their specific areas of responsibility as they negotiate with their school boards and community on ways to conceptually and financially support the ideas and resources needed for students' learning. Superintendents depend on their entrepreneurial, visionary, managerial, and interpersonal skills to respond to constant political, economic, and social changes in their districts. Changing demographics, diversity, and the divide between the haves and the have-nots are major challenges for suburban superintendents. While they have the authority to address such challenges, it is just not that easy.

Principals, as middle managers within their districts, set the tone for their schools as they implement the district's vision for educating students while accounting for the uniqueness of their school community. They are considered executives with the most influence over the work of teachers. They are the ones who usually lead school change (Howley et al., 1999). Principals responsible for schools that have changed and continue to change demographically face unique challenges in helping themselves and others accommodate a new type of community that requires new ways of thinking and different types of resources to ensure every student's opportunity to learn. Challenges vary from school to school because of school demographics, teacher characteristics, and program differences.

Student Achievement in Relation to National and State Mandates

Suburban superintendents have had the luxury of being able to boast about their students' achievement, as reflected in their standardized test scores, college acceptance rates, merit scholarships, and advanced placement scores. Increasing numbers of low-achieving students have resulted in a concern about low test scores and dropout, graduation, and retention rates. As a result, an achievement gap has emerged. According to the National Governors' Association, the achievement gap is about race and class because there is a gap in achievement between minority and disadvantaged students and white students. The gap is not just with standardized test scores. The gap exists with dropout rates; advanced placement exams; honors, advanced placement, and gifted classes; and college acceptance rates (Ladson-Billings, 2006).

A focus on the achievement gap in the suburbs became particularly acute with the emergence of the No Child Left Behind (NCLB) Act of 2001, which required school districts to report and use high-stakes test scores for different student groups to bring about achievement gains. NCLB has had a signature requirement that schools make adequate yearly progress to ensure that all students reach proficiency in reading and mathematics by 2014. However, with changes in the national political landscape, this requirement in the Elementary and Secondary Education Act may be dropped in favor of requiring districts to meet college- and career-ready standards. States also are being asked to come up with systems that pinpoint how well teachers and principals are doing to close the achievement gap. With this new incentive, principals are being judged first and foremost by their teachers' success on improving students' standardized test scores. Like other district administrators, suburban superintendents know that decisions about their districts have been and will continue to be determined by their high-stakes test results.

The achievement gap has perpetuated itself, with minorities and disadvantaged students being overrepresented in low-track classes. Bedford superintendent Jere Hochman asks, if you have 21 percent Hispanic students in a predominantly white school district, why are there not 21 percent of calculus classes, art classes, and the soccer team filled with Hispanic students (Hochman, 2009)? Socioeconomic status (SES) has been found to affect track assignments as well. A highly proficient student from a low socioeconomic background has only a 50–50 chance of being placed in a high-track class (Burris & Welner, 2005).

Different philosophies, curricula, and instructional practices have been and continue to be tried to close the achievement gap, from heterogeneous grouping to Sheltered Instruction Observation Protocol (SIOP) to culturally responsive curricula. Different district superintendents have developed their own formulas for making changes, based on their philosophies, experiences, and sociopolitical needs.

Funding

Funding in suburban districts has become a major issue because of the economy. Suburban superintendents are dependent on their local communities to pass budgets to help fund school district expenses. Increased unemployment and a depressed housing market have affected the way in which local residents vote for the district budget because they simply do not want to pay higher taxes, especially if their own children are not taking advantage of the local public schools. Just recently we heard about a public official who shared on national television his concern about paying taxes for his local public schools when his own children were going to private school. These conditions and attitudes are creating untenable financial situations for superintendents to the point where programs are being eliminated and personnel are being cut. One superintendent, committed to joining one of the networks mentioned in Chapter 1, does not have the fee required for membership. As he explained, he has had to cut positions this past year and could not justify the expenditure.

Personnel Issues

The biggest challenge for school leaders in changing suburban schools is the nearly all-white teaching staff responsible for teaching an increasing number of minority students. We hear numbers such as 85 percent minority students and 96 percent white teaching staff who have worked in the district for twenty-two years or more and have hostile and resistant attitudes that are difficult to change. One scenario has principals handing out school supplies for kids to do their homework while teachers are making comments such as, "Whoa, how come they say they're poverty, but they're walking in with the gym shoes that cost $100?" (Lutton, 2009).

School leaders know that teachers need to change their attitudes, beliefs, expectations, and practices and stop blaming students and their families for gaps in academic achievement (Howard, 2007). Instead, they need to meet children where they are. It is not just about teaching the fifth-grade curriculum but rather making personal connections with students. Teachers need to learn about students' family culture and interests and use their relationships to reinforce academic development.

Community Issues

Suburban school district leaders are faced with a complex set of community issues. At one extreme are the parents who have been in the district and expect schools to deliver the way they did in the past. At the other extreme are immigrant parents, possibly undocumented, who do not want to interact with the schools because of fear of being deported. There also are those parents who, while representing minority populations, are vocal about expecting schools to deliver for their children as well. Witness such changes in the schools as bilingual teachers, bilingual materials, and bilingual psychologists. Parents communicate how they expect to see additional multicultural authors in kids' backpacks and some different songs at the music concert that reflect the identity kids bring to school (Lutton, 2009). Past and current demographics determine the community composition and affect the types and levels of parental involvement, which directly affect the roles and responsibilities of the leaders.

Professional and Personal Challenges

Sitting superintendents, accustomed to leading historically high-achieving districts, need to alter their own thinking and behavior because they now are responsible for students and communities with vastly different racial, educational, linguistic, and socioeconomic backgrounds. The district's reputation might change as increasing levels of poverty set in and wealthier families send their children to private and parochial schools. Sitting superintendents also need to adapt to possible changes on their school boards as increasing numbers of minority families want representation on how the schools are run. New superintendents need to be aware of the complexities associated with changing demographics and be prepared professionally and personally to respond sensitively and proactively to both the *old guard* and the *new guard.*

Sitting principals, often accustomed to working with the same teachers for twenty years or more, must transform themselves rather quickly to be able to serve as role models for their staff, so that together they can make the necessary changes with curriculum, instruction, and assessment to meet varying students' needs. New principals, while not emotionally involved with historical patterns of behavior, need to know how to navigate and blend the old with the new so that all are committed to and involved with what is rather than what was.

There are definite professional and personal challenges for school leaders who have been in their districts for long periods of time who have seen in subtle and not-so-subtle ways an erosion of their status quo. They probably are being challenged by their board, community, and staff about their ability to lead as successfully as they did in the past, and they probably are questioning themselves in a similar vein.

They identified with one type of district or school when they began and now must adjust to different external and internal pressures of accountability and might be at a loss for how to ensure success for all.

School leaders new to their positions have different challenges because they need to be cognitively and socially skilled at honoring and perpetuating a community's history while bringing the entire district or school together into a new age of multicultural coexistence and collaboration. For both experienced and new leaders in changing suburban school districts, the professional and personal challenges cannot be underestimated.

Mimi Padovan, Principal of Galloway Ridge Intermediate School in Columbus, Ohio, knows only too well about adjusting to changes in her school building. Since assuming the role ten years ago as principal for approximately 650 fifth- and sixth-grade students, Mimi has seen free and reduced lunch participation climb from 35 percent to more than 70 percent. One-fourth to one-third of her students are either English language learners (ELLs) or special education students, with more than a few special education students coming from her ELL student population. With an increase in the number of economically disadvantaged families in the school's surrounding community, many of her students move from one school to the next and back again and may have only one parent at home. In fact, more and more of her students are being raised by their grandparents. Student absenteeism is also a chronic challenge. She has even purchased alarm clocks for a few of her students so that they can make it to the school bus on time. See Mimi's thoughts about working with teachers in Box 2.1.

Box 2.1 From the Principal's Desk on Working With Teachers

Principal Mimi Padovan has a lot of strategies for helping get her students to school so they have ample opportunity to learn. Mimi has instilled in her teaching staff the idea that they cannot engage in the blame game. Recycling lesson plans and "I taught it, but they didn't learn it" simply will not work. Rather, teachers work together to figure out how to best provide a changing student population with a quality education so that they can be successful in 21st century America. Mimi knows how lucky she is to have a hardworking teaching staff that is committed to all of the students. She knows that they can go elsewhere where the workload may be less demanding, but they want to stay where they are able to work alongside her in educating each and every one of their students for their future. (M. Padovan, personal communication, June 16, 2011)

Mimi's school has gone from being on *academic watch* to being *effective* and *excellent,* on its local report card from the Ohio Department of Education. Even though some of her students have not passed all of the assessment indicators, many of them have shown more than the expected growth in a year on standardized tests. She also is quite pleased that her sixth-grade students have passed the reading and mathematics tests and continues to work on the same strategies with her fifth-grade students.

What is it about Mimi, as a principal, that enables her to see her school's challenges as opportunities for success? She truly is an instructional leader who, as she readily admits, is driven toward excellence so students have the best opportunities to succeed. She focuses on four key elements that permeate the culture of Galloway Ridge:

1. *Collaboration* is a must. She expects teachers to collaborate on the instruction and assessment of students. Particularly important is teachers' collaboration around best practices: teaching key vocabulary, front-loading concepts, providing descriptive and specific feedback, checking daily for understanding, and giving students an opportunity to redo work to improve. She gets excited talking about the way in which teachers in the building develop their own ideas for collaboration. For example, a group of special education teachers developed a method in which to cross-group students during intervention time—a daily period established for teachers to work individually or with small groups on skill development—so that students with specific needs are able to work with students with similar needs from other classrooms.

2. *Goal setting* is critical for bringing about change. She and the staff set a goal that they would meet adequate yearly progress, as required by the federal No Child Left Behind Act, and help all students be successful to meet this goal. Students stay with the same teacher for both fifth and sixth grades to promote a sense of stability and continuity for both students and teachers.

3. *Data-driven decision-making processes* create opportunities for focused intervention. She believes that teachers need to collaborate on the review of student test results and develop individualized intervention strategies for students to help them with specific skill levels.

4. *Personal reflection and professional development* promote growth. Every year, teachers self-report on their use of research-based

practices, their collaborative and coteaching practices, and their assessment practices. They use these self-reports to reflect on their progress with students and develop goals for their students and themselves. Teachers also engage in professional development through whole-school seminars or meetings and small-group work sessions. Mimi facilitates one all-school seminar each month. She and the teachers discuss articles and book chapters and utilize the same type of instructional techniques (e.g., jigsaw method) that she expects teachers to use in their classrooms. Well versed on research-based practices, she makes it a point to help teachers stay current with practices that apply to their student population. Each week, she writes a newsletter that highlights a synopsis of a research-based practice.

Guidelines for Succeeding in Changing Suburban School Districts

- Assess your own belief system and know yourself
- Engage in environmental scans to understand changes
- Reaffirm existing relationships and form new ones
- Collaboratively develop a plan of action that acknowledges changes
- Monitor progress

As a result of the challenges facing many of the students, both inside and outside the classroom, it becomes evident that Mimi's daily life as a principal is much more difficult today than it was when she began. She and the staff do not have all of the answers, but they do have a desire to work together to design methods to effectively educate their students. As the educational leader of her building, Mimi has created a culture that enables her colleagues to collaborate on tactics to reach their goals (M. Padovan, personal communication, June 16, 2011).

Guidelines for Succeeding in Changing Suburban School Districts

Like Mimi Padovan, school leaders are beginning to share their stories on ways that they have changed themselves, their districts, and their schools to accommodate their increasingly diverse student populations. Some examples are incorporated below as five basic guidelines are offered. See Figure 2.1 for the major purpose of each guideline.

Assess Your Own Belief System and Know Yourself

School leaders need to truly appreciate and believe in their school districts and stakeholders. They should want to advocate for

Figure 2.1 Five Basic Guidelines for Succeeding in Changing
Suburban Schools

Guideline	Purpose
Assess your own belief system and know yourself	Helps with credibility and vision
Engage in environmental scans to understand changes	Helps to plan
Reaffirm existing relationships and form new ones	Helps to accomplish goals
Collaboratively develop a plan of action that acknowledges changes	Helps with short- and long-range accomplishments
Monitor progress	Helps to determine plan's validity and reliability

opportunities for all students, even if it means losing some political capital along the way. As privileged districts begin to lose their ranking and financial advantages, school leaders should instinctively want to fight for the school's ability to help all students succeed, even if it means working longer and harder to make slower than usual progress.

School leaders need to ask themselves the following:

1. In what ways do I show that I care about making changes in my school or district?

2. How am I demonstrating that I am psychologically, socially, and cognitively prepared to face the challenges that accompany a changing student population?

3. In what ways can I serve as an exemplary role model for my staff, students, and community to create a paradigm shift that fully supports an increasingly diverse student population?

If school leaders can provide specific and concrete ideas for these three questions, they probably have the wherewithal to serve as visionary change agents for their schools and districts. These are leaders who have trust in themselves and others, are willing and able to change, have the strength to confront inequities head-on, and strive toward harmony in the face of major differences. They are not afraid to take the heat from any one group, including local and state government, and are capable of listening earnestly to all constituencies as they work toward improvement.

If school leaders have difficulty in generating ideas for the three questions above, it obviously is best to admit this before losing oneself and the students to halfhearted attempts to adjust to a changing student population.

One suburban superintendent, concerned mostly with declining test scores, went about it the wrong way with her principals. Rather than truly studying each school's profile, she commanded the principals to raise test scores by the next test cycle. The principals began to confide in each other about the superintendent's expectations and realized that they were being bullied to do what they perceived to be the impossible. They did not have enough time to study trend data, identify the source of the problems, work collaboratively with teachers, or put into place additional resources for their increasing number of struggling learners. These principals had seen a surge of free and reduced lunch needs in the past five years and, while not exactly sure about the impact of such changes, knew from their teachers and test results that there were serious achievement gaps. This superintendent was too concerned about public perception to allow herself or her administrative staff to honestly acknowledge and seriously address the district's real student population. She has since left the district because she was not equipped to address the challenges that accompany a changing student population.

School leaders who have been successful are seen as credible change agents because of their focus on bridging the achievement gap in their schools and communities (Leverett, 2011). They have a message that fits the evolving nature of the schools and district and believe in their message. See Superintendent Jere Hochman's message in Box 2.2.

Box 2.2   From the Superintendent's Desk on Conveying a Message About His Beliefs

Jere Hochman, the superintendent mentioned earlier, conveys daily that, "It is still all about the kids—every single one of them—every single day" (Hochman, 2009, p. 1) because he wants everyone in the district to know that it is about providing the best education possible for all students. He couples this message with his own optimism that his district will see the achievement gap close because of his belief in his remarkable adults in the school district (including teachers, custodians, bus drivers . . . everyone), motivated students and families and community participants. (J. Hochman, personal communication, August 8, 2011)

Engage in Environmental Scans to Understand Changes

School leaders need to know what they are talking about. Proclamations about closing the achievement gap need to be supported by data about the actual gap. Declarations about transforming schools and districts to be culturally proficient need to be backed with current performance indicators. Data need to be gathered about the educational context in which these claims are made.

Knowing and understanding a school district comes from a school leader's analysis of how well the organization is functioning and what it needs to improve. An analysis yields information and provides direction for an institution. A high school principal might discover that he needs to do something to counter the high rate of absenteeism and dropouts with his African American females.

Conducting environmental scans, whether formally or informally, helps leaders to determine an organization's strengths and weaknesses. Environmental scans consider the factors that will influence the direction and goals of an organization. They are a process of gathering and analyzing both factual and subjective information about the internal and external environment to identify opportunities and threats (Cool Avenues, n.d.; Environmental Scanning, n.d.; Pashiardis, 1996; Popovics, 1990).

One type of scan is a strengths, weaknesses, opportunities, and threats (SWOT) analysis. Developed by Albert Humphrey at the Stanford Research Institute, SWOT analysis enables a leader to use a readily available inventory of contextually based needs to plan strategically for an organization. Figure 2.2 identifies questions typically asked during a SWOT analysis (Immigrate to Manitoba, Canada, n.d.; Wepner, 2011).

Figure 2.2   Questions for a SWOT Analysis

Strengths	Weaknesses
• What does your institution do well? • What unique resources do you have? • What do others see as your strengths?	• What could you improve? • Where do you have fewer resources than other institutions? • What do others see as your weaknesses?
Opportunities	Threats
• What good opportunities are available to you? • What trends would you take advantage of? • How can you turn your strengths into opportunities?	• What trends could affect you negatively? • What are competing institutions doing? • How would a weakness be potential threat?

A SWOT analysis for a changing suburban district or school would be able to reveal the perceived strengths and weaknesses of a district and, more important, what is helping and holding back teachers from assisting all of their students to achieve at acceptable levels. Here's an example of a SWOT analysis conducted by an elementary principal with her staff (see Figure 2.3). This SWOT analysis helped the staff see clearly what they had and did not have. It actually helped them realize that they do work in a good facility with dedicated colleagues, have help from a local university, and have put into practice certain programs that are beginning to succeed. They also came to realize that, with increasing numbers of culturally and linguistically diverse students, they need to better understand how to reach out to more and more students and their parents; otherwise, they are looking at possibly losing their colleagues because of unacceptable achievement gains. This analysis helped the staff to better understand what needed to be done to build on what already had been accomplished.

Figure 2.3   Example of a SWOT Analysis in a Changing Suburban Elementary School

Strengths	Weaknesses
• Dedicated teaching staff • Strong leadership team • Collaborative work across grade levels • School building is in mint condition • Schoolwide incentives to read • After-school tutoring program • Students come from the local university to help with tutoring, small-group instruction, and an after-school program	• Minority students' reading standardized test scores • Parent involvement • Technology • Lack of teaching assistants and literacy coaches • Lack of knowledge about culturally sensitive curriculum and instruction
Opportunities	Threats
• Bilingual program in primary grades is showing promise • New vice principal with Hispanic background can communicate effectively with parent community • University liaison with literacy background is available and interested in working with teachers on the reading program • Leadership team needs to reach out to immigrant and minority parents	• New statewide teacher evaluation system that is based on students' standardized reading scores will put teachers on warning • New principal evaluation system could affect principal's status • Immigrants continue to move into the neighborhood without legal status, knowledge of English, or gainful employment • Lack of parent involvement is hurting students' achievement

Reaffirm Existing Relationships and Form New Ones

School leaders need to be able to form relationships. In general, they need to work closely with key persons within and outside the organization; be responsive to critical persons in the overall organization; keep critical persons in the organization informed so that they are willing to support resources; and negotiate with key players to keep them appropriately involved, aware of and respectful of boundaries, and honest about their level of participation and contributions to the organization (Wepner, Hopkins, Johnson, & Damico, 2011).

Superintendents need to reaffirm and form relationships with all members of the community to help them recognize and value diversity. They need to have solid working relationships with school board members to provide the necessary resources to promote achievement for all students. Superintendents must build trust with staff members so that they will accept a district's direction for change. They also need to continue to develop and form new relationships with members of the community by attending athletic events and community-based programs and speaking at various civic and religious groups.

Principals need to form close working relationships with their staff so that they support the school and district mission. Principals need to have close ties with their parent organizations and parent community to ensure involvement and support. They need to have strong, positive relationships with their students so that their students feel connected. The principal's visibility and knowledge of students depends on the size of the school and the resources available for administrative oversight. Principals also need to have positive relationships with the custodial, cafeteria, and transportation staff so that they work alongside the principal to help students and staff with daily functioning.

Those already in such positions have established many relationships but now must reach out to different groups and some of the same stakeholders to help all those connected to the district understand that, with a more diverse student population, it cannot be business as usual. Those new to a district or school need to use their newness as an opportunity to listen and learn about the history and traditions of the schools and the perceived challenges of a demographically changed district.

A superintendent new to a district, yet seemingly familiar with changing suburban district needs from his previous position, realized too late that he alienated the teachers across the district because of his condescending views about the teachers' work ethic. He expressed to the teachers' union and his administrative staff that the teachers "were

Ideas for Superintendents and Principals on Developing Relationships

For superintendents

- Respond affirmatively to attend as many events as possible and offer to bring another staff person with you. This becomes mutually beneficial in the ability to firmly establish relationships with staff members and expose staff members to the district's internal and external community.
- Schedule one-on-one lunches with key members of the staff to get to know them in less formal settings.
- Schedule and hold sacred the opportunity to walk through buildings with the principal to meet the staff and students.
- Use scheduled meetings with administrative staff as a forum for the exchange of information, ideas, and reflective thoughts so that it is not just about business but also about the persons involved in overseeing the district and schools.
- Attend school-based faculty meetings to both share information and listen to faculty's thoughts, ideas, and concerns. Follow up with whatever you promise to pursue, especially concerns that are shared by many that can be resolved.

For principals

- Meet individually and informally with faculty to make connections beyond classroom observations and challenges.
- Attend after-school and evening events and meetings, especially those planned by teachers and the Parent-Teacher Association (PTA), to show support.
- Invite groups of faculty to have lunch periodically.
- Form a professional development book club with staff members.
- Attend student events and activities, from the arts to sports.
- Attend community events that involve members of your school.
- Use arrival, dismissal, and lunch as opportunities to chat with students, parents, and staff.

spoiled" and should stop complaining about the instructional issues that they were having with their culturally and linguistically diverse students. Unlike in his previous district, the teachers in this district still needed time and help to adjust to the new expectations placed upon them. Although his administrative team tried to help him understand some of the transitional challenges across the district, he did not listen. Eventually, he was asked to leave because he had not formed relationships that enabled him to be an effective leader at a critical time in the district's history.

It is easy to know that it is important to form relationships, but it is quite another thing to know how. Some ideas for both superintendents and principals are in the sidebar.

Collaboratively Develop a Plan of Action That Acknowledges Changes

As the good proverb says, "Failing to plan is planning to fail." School leaders need to work collaboratively with their administrators, teachers, staff, students, community, and board members to develop and implement a plan of action that accounts for racial and cultural differences and promotes a culture of success in closing the achievement gap.

Jerry Weast, former superintendent of Maryland's Montgomery County Public Schools, exemplified the power of planning to positively influence the direction of achievement for his district's increasing minority student population. Weast began by collecting data from test scores, interviews, and opinion polls from employees, parents, and the community that ended up highlighting the disparities between the white majority and the impoverished, limited-English minority students. He used the data to develop a Call to Action, which provided a blueprint for turning data into deliverables: an improved technology infrastructure that allowed for a web-based instructional management system, annual surveys, and annual reports about the district's progress; a professional development system for teachers, administrators, and support staff; and a living and breathing strategic plan. The success of his Call to Action reflected his ability to define the problem as accurately as possible and get support from his stakeholders.

Jerry Weast understood that, as the CEO, he had the ultimate responsibility to ensure educational equity and to close the achievement gap between student groups in his district. He established, through collaborative efforts, a plan that included nonnegotiable goals for achievement and instruction, as well as resources and assistance needed to accomplish the goals. His district's goals were based on an understanding of the root causes of the existing achievement gaps and an understanding of the different cultures in his district (Dillon, 2011). Leaders who succeed in meeting the needs of their changing student population have developed specific pathways to influence student outcomes, which includes nonnegotiable goals for achievement and high-quality instruction. Leaders usually focus on multifaceted curricular and instructional changes that are culturally relevant; that is, the programs and materials empower students to maintain and celebrate their cultural identity. Culturally relevant pedagogy, or the instruction provided by teachers, builds off students' lives and knowledge of their shared community so that students are not forced to give up their identity but rather use their own cultural referents to help them acquire knowledge, skills, and attitudes. When school leaders and teachers are aware of students' cultural lives and cultural experiences, they can take that knowledge and make a connection between what students' already know and understand and what is taught in the classroom (Teaching Tolerance, 2010). See Lead Teacher George Crute's thoughts on developing a plan in Box 2.3.

Box 2.3   From a Lead Teacher's Desk on Developing a Plan

George Crute, Lead Teacher for Professional Development in Bedford School District, Bedford, New York, acknowledges that changes in his district have been multifaceted. While his teachers believe deeply in wanting all students to succeed and work daily to figure out solutions, they have a very different perspective on teaching to accommodate individual student needs. As different curricular initiatives have been implemented to meet the needs of students, instructional approaches have also been altered. Bedford has developed a systematic approach for working with teachers so that they understand how to differentiate instruction in learner-active, technology-infused classrooms utilizing a ten principles approach. This approach includes analysis of formative- and summative-assessment measures to inform instruction. At the secondary level, he is helping teachers learn how to work with targeted groups of students through small-group instruction and individualized activities designed to enable student choice, all within technologically rich environments. Additionally, the district has developed a multitude of extras: an after-school homework helper club, a paid internship program for graduate students to provide additional support in the classroom, outside consultants to help teachers with their own self-reflective practices, and college visitations for middle school students who may never be afforded a first-time visit to a college campus. (G. Crute, personal communication, June 21, 2011)

Professional development for both administrators and teachers is critical to the success of a plan. Administrators need to be aware of current and anticipated changes and their implications for student achievement. They need to know what other schools and districts are doing, what is needed for their own schools and districts, and how to implement needed changes. Some superintendents actually conduct book studies with their leadership teams to help them glean such information. School and school district visitations, administrative retreats, outside consultants, coaching, conferences, minority student achievement networks, and regional, state, and national meetings help administrators with their own professional development. Any professional development opportunities need to be applied specifically to the needs of the schools and district.

Similar types of professional development opportunities should exist for teachers, with a focus on helping teachers appreciate and understand how to work directly with a changing student population. Classroom visitations, coaching, semiannual and annual retreats,

> ## Box 2.4   From the Principal's Desk on Conveying a Message About Her Beliefs
>
> As Rosa Taylor, principal of Park Avenue School in Port Chester, New York, explains, sometimes principals get caught in the middle of pushing teachers on multiple tasks without explaining why or how such tasks should be implemented. She discovered from her teachers that both superintendents and principals need to provide better communication about expected changes. She used her end-of-year retreat to have her teachers identify the issues and develop recommended strategies to improve the communication system in her district. (R. Taylor, personal communication, June 16, 2011)

workshops, teacher–university faculty collaborations, and conferences contribute to teachers' ability to envision, implement, and assess the value of new initiatives and strategies. Such professional development needs to be desired by teachers, not thrust upon them, when needed changes are made. See Principal Rosa Taylor's thoughts about communicating with teachers in Box 2.4.

Teachers themselves also can become part of a plan for providing professional development. These teachers can serve as role models for working successfully with minority students. For example, a high school African American English teacher consults with white teachers to help them become more aware of and inclined to use culturally sensitive practices. She also developed a multicultural writing program for the district (Sharp, 2003).

Another critical component of a plan must include working with the parent community to temper the discouragement of the establishment and encourage involvement of minority and immigrant newcomers. Such outreach can come from the schools themselves or in consultation with colleges and universities. Stanton Wortham from the University of Pennsylvania wrote about the New Latino Diaspora across the United States, with specific emphasis on a changing suburban school district in Norristown, Pennsylvania. A major focus of his work is on increased immigrant parental involvement in the schools by, for example, opening bilingual resource rooms at several elementary schools to make bilingual staff available to meet with parents and students after school on a weekly basis. This helps parents learn about teachers' expectations and create relationships with teachers and administrators so that they ultimately become more involved in the school. As one parent explained, he learned how to help his daughter with her homework only after the teacher worked with him (Education and the New Latino Diaspora, 2011).

As noted in the preface, the Changing Suburbs Institute has parent education as one of its goals and offers in concert with school districts an annual Hispanic Parents Leadership Institute held entirely in Spanish to help parents learn about the U.S. educational system so that they know how to be more involved in their children's education. See Chapter 8 for a full description of this institute.

A district's plans must balance the way in which resources are allocated so that all types of students benefit. As George Crute explained, the administrators know that they must provide services for struggling learners yet must also support enrichment resources for those who are accelerated. They have reached out to their community and local college to bring resources to the school that help provide relief, support, and new ideas to the teacher (G. Crute, personal communication, June 21, 2011).

A plan also needs to subscribe to the needs of the schools within a district. One district, with an even distribution of minority students in each elementary school, might implement a specific type of bilingual and literacy development program in each elementary school. Another district, with an impoverished south side of town and an affluent north side of town, would allocate its resources very differently so that only the impoverished elementary schools have the bilingual and specialized literacy programs. This latter district would have to invest more heavily into developing culturally sensitive programs at the middle school level to promote student and parent coexistence.

While the basic elements of a plan are the same (curriculum, instruction, assessment, professional development, parent education, materials, technology), its uniqueness is driven by the type and degree of changes in the community. Once a plan is developed to meet the needs of the specific types of students, it needs to be marketed widely and deeply so that it is accepted by the community as a way to focus on all students.

Monitor Progress

The only way to know if a plan is working is to monitor progress. Jerry Weast, described above, knew that his plan was working because student achievement had become evident. For example, African American and Hispanic students on free and reduced lunch are now taking at least one advanced placement exam (Dillon, 2011).

Progress should be monitored with all components of the plan, from curriculum implementation to student achievement on standardized tests. Progress does not just mean dramatic results on standardized tests. It means that there is evidence of steady changes in curriculum implementation, teacher instruction, parent involvement, and student achievement. For example, an elementary principal was quite delighted when she saw two important changes in her fourth-grade classrooms. Teachers who had been working with a faculty member from a local college on mathematics instruction were teaching differently and, as a result, saw students' mathematics scores on the district's unit tests improve. A middle school principal was pleased with the progress in his school when the language arts teachers, previously resistant to individualized learning centers for writing, began to use them to focus on specific writing needs. A high school principal whose students could not pass the statewide mathematics test passed after working in an after-school math clinic run by graduate students in mathematics education.

Records must be kept of students' progress so that both teachers and administrators know what programs and instructional strategies are working or not working. The key is to monitor and evaluate constantly so that programs that are not successful over a period of time can be eliminated while those that are successful can be maintained and improved.

Concluding Remarks

It can no longer be a blame game. It is what it is. Suburban school districts have changed and will continue to change with increasing numbers of students with racial, ethnic, linguistic, and socioeconomic differences. Accommodating such changes cannot be done in isolation. School leaders must work collaboratively with their constituencies to own the situation and welcome the opportunity to help students and their parents get what they rightly deserve from the public schools. School leaders need to know and believe in their own message, truly understand their schools and community, work closely with their stakeholders, formulate doable and progressive plans, and monitor the health of their plans so that their students are developing appropriately and enthusiastically.

Part II

Addressing the Challenges of Changing Suburban School Districts

3

Changing the Culture of the School

Felix Flores started his career as a teacher in a large urban district. After thirteen years of urban school service, married with twins on the way, he thought he would try the suburbs to be closer to his home. Fourteen years later, his vision of the suburbs is sharpened. Now as principal of one of the Changing Suburbs Institute elementary-level professional development schools, he sees that the true story of today's suburban community is very complicated. Leading a school that has moved to dual language bilingual programming as a central strategy for closing the achievement gap of Latino students, compared to their white counterparts, Felix is deeply aware of the challenges of helping to build a caring school environment that is focused on student achievement and is honest about the stories data can tell. While children from well-established, middle-class Latino families do well in his school, he is worried about new immigrants and males from diverse backgrounds as statewide assessment scores for those groups revealed gaps compared to the scores of white students and females from diverse backgrounds. Felix works with the building leadership team, professional development school liaison, community partners, teachers, parents, and others to develop a community of care and support for all. All voices are heard and focused on solutions and progress.

School leaders need to acknowledge and change the culture of their schools and districts so that their teachers and their school community can have a positive impact on students' learning. This chapter describes ways in which school leaders have been able to change their schools and districts and presents specific classroom examples with tools to use and guidelines for such changes.

Opportunities and Challenges of Increasing Diversity in the Schools

Twenty-one percent of all children enrolled in American public schools speak a language other than English at home (U.S. Census Bureau, 2009). These linguistically diverse students are immigrants, children of immigrants, and American-born citizens. To consider the enormity of the issues at hand, it is critical to realize that thirty-five percent of all children enrolled in American public schools have at least one foreign-born parent (Nieto, 2009). The United States has built its success on integrating immigrants into schools and the greater community. For many years this was a largely urban project. However, in the 21st century, and as discussed in the previous chapters, there is a dramatic shift in the settlement patterns for immigrant groups and ethnic communities. They have moved to the suburbs. Looking for safety and work, new and settled immigrant groups are being attracted by the suburbs. Additionally, suburbs were historically wealthier than their urban counterparts; however, poverty is now an emerging issue in suburban districts as well. These new settlement patterns require second-order change in our schools (Shannon & Bylsma, 2007). New ways of teaching and engaging the community are required as schools must shift and be transformed (Banks et al., 2005). These shifts bring forth challenges and opportunities to suburban school leaders.

Responsibilities of School Leaders

As school demographics and communities change, administrators must integrate new ideas into their daily and long-term approaches to learning and teaching, parent involvement, and language orientations. As school populations change, school leaders need to become familiar with a wider range of language teaching tools and become aware of international models of education so they are better able to support teachers to understand what educational experiences students may have had before coming to the United

States. They also need to understand the experiences of parents who have been educated abroad and their expectations of American schools. Further, school leaders need to understand the experiences, challenges, and successes of the diverse students in their schools.

Responsibilities of Teaching Staff

Teaching staff must expand their visions of family, what being educated means, and the range of ways we can engage families in education. For example, when Latino parents discuss wanting their children to be well educated, or in Spanish *buen educado,* this is really a focus on being well mannered and a good friend at school (Lang, Gómez, & Lasser, 2009; Valdes, 1996; Valdes, Capitelli, & Alvarez, 2011). Latino parents do want their children to be skilled and knowledgeable, but the words surrounding that idea are different. Additionally, American schools are generally focused on individual achievement. Within many immigrant communities there is more focus on group achievement and maintenance of the community (Valdes, 1996). These competing notions of the context for achievement may cause challenges as we strive to engage all in meaningful schooling. Further, teachers may need to include teaching strategies such as content area front loading, explicit teaching of vocabulary, and hands-on experiences with language experience overlays in order to teach students. These strategies have been shown to improve achievement for English language learners and may also help English-proficient immigrants and children of immigrants.

Teachers should also include in their teaching programs across all subject areas lessons and units about understanding and accepting cultural and linguistic diversity (Lindquist, 2002). These lessons should be designed for all school students. If we are to change school culture and encourage the support of all students, then all students need to be part of this transformation. Students will be better able to participate in democratic schooling in a diverse society if we embrace the social studies as a means to develop cultural and social acceptance and knowledge (National Council for the Social Studies, 1994). This is especially true in schools in the changing suburbs. Some interesting examples of teaching and learning activities centered on cultural acceptance and knowledge include experiences where school staff (administrators, teachers, and staff) have participated in teaching tolerance days with students, literature units that emphasize culture as a lens for literary critique, and elementary school units focused on aspects of culture that are universal (language, housing, transportation, family) and support students to see cross-cultural similarities and differences.

Responsibilities of School Community

The larger school may include nonprofit agencies, school support entities such as a parent-teacher associations (PTAs) or parent-teacher organizations (PTOs), and universities. Nonprofit agencies such as the YMCA, YWCA, Jewish Community Center (JCC), Boys and Girls Clubs, the Lions, and others, such as local arts groups, can provide significant support to changing suburban schools. Within the Changing Suburbs Institute network, arts groups are providing during-school and after-school arts programming that provide another way for English language learners to connect with English, school, and American culture. Arts programs, in particular, are beneficial as English is learned secondary to the arts experience and is engaging and enjoyable for the students. Music programs have historically been a successful way of integrating new Americans into the gorgeous mosaic that is our modern society. In the changing suburbs, there are drumming programs, choral experiences, and school community dance troupes that encourage children to excel in nonverbal expression. Low-cost and free music programs such as those offered in settlement houses in our urban centers now can be agents of change in the suburbs as well. Immigrants participating in free music programs offered by community groups have earned seats in the New York Philharmonic as adults. Providing voice to immigrants though music is a very positive approach.

Within two of our Changing Suburbs Institute professional development school districts, a grant provided by a local film arts center allowed students to create digitally animated films with sound tracks. The students worked after school to develop the stories and animate and produce their films. A red carpet opening night was held at the center's Arts Cineplex. Teacher candidates from the college worked as tutors within the film workshops at the professional development schools and provided at-the-elbow language support, allowing the elementary students to achieve as junior filmmakers. The community, families, school staff, and students were treated to viewing the students' monolingual and bilingual stories on the big screen. An arts approach to integrating children of immigrants is an effective strategy for developing skills and intellectual prowess that serve children through their education and beyond.

PTAs and PTOs often support parent-education programming. Throughout the Changing Suburbs Institute network, active PTAs work to enrich students' experiences at schools through organizing and funding arts, interactive literacy, and field-trip programs. At three of our professional development schools in the Changing Suburbs

Institute network, PTAs are responsible for parent-education workshops and outreach to new parents. Some of the topics covered are district resources and orientation, homework, getting ready for parent–teacher conferences, and college preparation. In one of our Changing Suburbs districts, a private donor and the PTA give a gift of picture books to every baby born in the local hospital that has an in-district address. This early contact with families helps establish reading as a family priority and a positive connection with the school district. Finally, public libraries are critical partners in this work. In all of our Changing Suburbs Institute districts, the public libraries collaborate with the district and provide books and computer services in languages other than English. The libraries also provide summer reading programs for children, grades pre-K through 12. Additionally, libraries are providing English as a second language classes for parents.

School-wide communities can also be enriched with resources from groups such as local neighborhood associations, cultural clubs, and nonprofit agencies. These community resources may be drawn on to provide academic, social, and health supports. As schools seek to address more issues that recent immigrants may have accessing and interpreting American education, it may be necessary to reach out to new partners to provide the wide range of supports required for school success.

Ways in Which Teachers and Schools Are Changing to Accommodate Increasing Diversity

Accommodating increasing diversity requires an openness to change. Teachers and school staff need to be ready to learn and be flexible in their interactions and thinking. Many changes are noticeable in schools with diversity on the rise where the staff is genuinely investing in teaching the children who are enrolled.

Examples of Changes in Teachers and Schools

Elementary schools. At a medium-sized professional development school, teachers started to notice that, as they screened children for kindergarten, more and more children were not coming from nursery school but from home-based child care with relatives. They began to think that recent classes of incoming kindergarteners had less knowledge of the alphabet, shapes, and colors. They contacted the principal about this hunch and were able to write a staff development grant to conduct an action research project addressing this question and concern. After six months of study, they determined that, as the percentage of new immigrants increased in the incoming kindergarten classes, the percentage of the kindergarteners with schooling prior to kindergarten was also decreasing. In order to remedy the problem, they developed a kindergarten readiness program and parent-education workshop on basic literacy. All of the children who were identified as not having been in school yet and had low kindergarten readiness scores were invited to the program. Over a three-year period the kindergarten teachers were able to level the playing field and avoid kindergarten achievement gaps. (See Chapter 5 for additional details about this program.)

In one of the Changing Suburbs schools, special educators noticed that elementary-level children with disabilities who were also immigrants or children of immigrants often found making friends and integrating into the school-wide community difficult. The special educators and general education teachers joined together and developed a program called Reading Buddies. This program partnered immigrant children enrolled in special education with general education students (some immigrants and some native born) for ten weeks of short (thirty minutes) but daily reading visits. The children were assigned partners and read their independent reading books to each other. Prior to the reading visits, training was provided to the general education students about disability studies, supporting a developing reader, diversity, and being a good friend. At the end of the ten-week sessions, children had formed friendships and were more welcoming and accepting of each other at recess, at lunch, and in the community beyond school.

In another professional development school partner district, an informal program called the Second Cup of Coffee was implemented. This free program allowed parents to stay in school after they dropped off their children and have informal conversations about schooling. Sometimes the professional development school liaison presented a concept or activities; other times teachers, student teachers, special area teachers, and the school social worker participated. A safe place to connect with teachers and school support was created to orient parents to American schools.

Middle schools/junior high schools. Addressing aspirations is critical at this developmental stage. Particularly for children of immigrants, it is important to have support to help students stay motivated to study and do well academically. With the professional development school network, many of the schools have access to minority achievement programs that help identify high-achieving students from diverse backgrounds and prepare college preparatory, academic, and social experiences. Students can also participate in college and career awareness events at their schools and visit campuses. The feedback on this type of programming has been very positive, indicating that the students were developing ideas about themselves as potential college students. Middle school students commented on how cozy the college library was, that they could see themselves attending college in a place like this, and that "it must be fun to live in the dorms and go to school with your friends!" As explained in the preface, the partnership agreements between Changing Suburbs Institute and the school districts provides a 50 percent discount to high school students who get accepted to the college. This represents a very significant investment on the part of the college to make higher education accessible to immigrants and children of immigrants.

Within the professional development school network, we have graduate students who have taken course work that address issues of education in the changing suburbs who serve as teaching interns. These interns provide a low cost but quality resource for students. Teaching interns serve as substitute teachers when needed but are in the school every day tutoring, building relationships, and providing homework help. By having the culturally and educationally attuned interns in the building every day, a strong community of support is built for adolescents with diverse cultural experiences and backgrounds.

High schools. At the high school level, support for high-achieving students from diverse backgrounds remains important. Within the Changing Suburbs Institute professional development schools network there is a minority achievement program at one of our high schools. This program provides extra classes and enrichment of English language learners who demonstrate academic giftedness. The program helps bridge the experience gap between that of new immigrant parents and established parents and provides a pathway to acceptance into advanced placement classes and highly selective college programs.

Support for students who have arrived in the United States during high school is critical as they are at a very high risk of school failure. In one of the Changing Suburbs Institute districts, they hire recent new immigrant high school graduates to be community-support workers. While attending a local community college, these high school graduates serve as role models and provide mentoring. One district noted that teen pregnancy and dropping out of high school were very prevalent with new arrivals prior to deployment of the community-support workers. With the community-support workers in place, teen pregnancy rates dropped slightly, and becoming pregnant was no longer a legitimate reason for dropping out. The community-support workers helped teen mothers access community resources and day care. The workers helped teen mothers complete high school by providing academic and organizational support. Interestingly, one of these teen mothers was accepted to Manhattanville College for her undergraduate studies, stayed with us for graduate school, student taught in a professional development school (where her daughter was enrolled), and recently was hired as an elementary teacher. Given thoughtful, caring, and rich academic support from teachers, staff, and administrators, diverse learners can be very successful.

Creating a School Culture That Works

The work of Thomas Sergiovanni (1999, 2009) highlights and explains the importance of community in schooling. The most successful schools provide a home away from home and a place to be someone who belongs and has something to contribute. This philosophy must be in place in a school that is changing and becoming more diverse.

Building Trust

One of the major strategies for building trust is full communication. Full communication in a diverse community is not only a paper- and text-driven endeavor. In full-communication schools, communication is in the bulletins of student work, on every piece of student work that goes home, in conversations during drop-off and dismissal, over the phone, in e-mail messages, and at meetings. Verbal communication in the parents' native language and in English is highly critical. Even for an immigrant parent who is fluent in English, formal school documents can be hard to interpret. Trust is built from care and a strong commitment to sharing and listening to ideas and information.

Engaging Personal Culture

As diversity increases, it needs to be honored and present in each interaction, lesson, and school day. The trivializing culture-of-the-day approach to multiculturalism that Sonia Nieto (2010) and James Banks (2001, 2004) criticize must be replaced by a culture that respects individuals and cultural differences and similarities. This all-cultures approach opens our eyes to a range of practices and visions of the good life. This widening vision allows us to embrace each child and family and support them in getting the benefit of public school education.

Another way to engage the cultural insights and experiences of the children is to create acculturation groups. These small groups meet with the school principal, assistant principal, or school social worker. During the group meetings, which are often held at lunchtime, school leaders talk openly with recent immigrants about the dimension of the new culture the students find notable or challenging. The purpose is to have thoughtful cross-cultural conversations and help make the transition to a new school and new culture more intentional and positive.

Confronting Issues of Social Dominance and Social Justice

Social justice is an essential perspective when designating programs and curricula for increasingly diverse schools. Are the materials being used representative of all in the building? Do classroom libraries include multicultural literature so that diverse students do not feel marginalized? Is instruction designed to be critical and support children to see issues from a range of perspectives? Can students address issues of race, ethnicity, and class in their studies? These ideas must be fully addressed.

Transforming Instructional Practices

Transformation is a process. However as a school changes, depending on the rate of the demographic shift, it may be necessary to respond quickly in an environment that is shifting. Waiting for the demographics to settle down may cause a school to do a great disservice to itself. Transformation in changing suburbs requires flexibility, the ability to access academic and social demographic data, and a willingness to respond actively and caringly. Action research is a key approach. (See Chapter 4 for additional information on action research as a form of professional development.) It allows educators to address specific dimensions of the changing school environment to address questions such as, do dual language students tend to drop out prior to middle school? Can using direct instruction of vocabulary increase learning key concepts in social studies? Does holding parent workshops on homework support improve the quality and amount of homework completed?

Recently one of the teachers within the Changing Suburbs Institute network conducted an action research project to understand his incoming students' language landscapes. Based on his preassessment of the class, he plans to use a great deal of Readers Theater to support the transition to the new school year. Readers Theater is a method of sharing stories or books in play format with dramatic in-character readings and dramatizations to bring the literature alive. This teaching strategy deployment was based on insights from the teacher's action research. Using action research as an anchor for figuring out what one's students need to be successful students is a critical approach in changing suburban contexts. Chase Young and Timothy Rasinski (2009) confirm that Readers Theater is a strong approach for encouraging English language learners in improving their fluency and interest in reading.

Hosting field-based curriculum methods courses at the professional development schools during the regular school day is another approach that brings state-of-the-art, research-based pedagogy alive for prospective and practicing teachers (Lang & Siry, 2008; Siry & Lang, 2010). Currently, professors collaborate with classroom teachers to provide courses that include seminars and scaffolded teaching experiences in literacy, English, social studies, science, math, assessment, and diversity using the Changing Suburbs classrooms as teaching laboratories for teacher candidates to develop their teaching repertoire, with professors and classroom teachers acting as guides. The children who participate get to see that even teachers learn, meet college students, and interact with professors. Finally, job-embedded staff development is provided for the classroom teachers within this approach.

Engaging the Entire School Community

One step toward engaging the whole community is to have a weekly bulletin that not only explains the details of the week but also celebrates progress toward schoolwide goals and contributions from all school community members (for example, clerical staff, special services, teachers, students, volunteers, parents, and community partners). Another important strategy is to have schoolwide events to bring the entire community together. Across the Changing Suburbs network, our student teachers are required to design, conduct, and present parent outreach workshops. Some of these events are smaller in scope and focus on very specific topics such as low-cost summer learning opportunities or reading strategies, while other workshops are broader in scope and are schoolwide, such as the Parent Literacy Connection Workshops or Family Math Nights. In one of our

Changing Suburbs Institute professional development schools, the school leader has Interest Days twice a year for the entire school. All staff members run a workshop about something they love: birding, singing, pottery, drum improvisation, poetry, collecting stamps, etc. The students sign up for two workshops they find interesting. With all adults in the building running a workshop, each workshop has only ten to twelve students in it. Adults and youngsters connect around interests that would otherwise not be possible, thereby building authentic interest-related bonds that bind the school community.

Guidelines for Creating and Sustaining a Culture That Works

Develop Self-Reflective Practices

Digital-journaling and digital-storytelling practices help all involved reflect on successes and challenges. Having a shared internal e-reflection site supports engagement. Some schools have a staff-only e-discussion board. Our Changing Suburbs Institute professional development schools' summer and year-end retreats help staff reflect on the development of the school program and how student and educator learning are being continuously improved.

Work Within and Across Cultures

At one of the elementary professional development schools, the principal starts the weekly message with two to three quotes from world leaders. Each week a different country and leader are featured. Through this practice the principal indicates to the staff that helpful insight comes from all corners of the earth. Working across and within cultures requires intentional action and support for ideas that may be unfamiliar.

Schooling is a highly culture-based endeavor. School leaders need to become aware of educational and schooling practice in other countries so they can be better prepared to take an international perspective when discussing American student and school issues with parents who have been educated abroad (Rong & Preissle, 2009). For example, most secondary school programs in Nordic countries do not assign and collect daily homework. Knowledge that expectations for

> **Guidelines for Creating and Sustaining a Culture That Works**
> - Develop self-reflective practices
> - Work within and across cultures
> - Promote communication practices
> - Assess climate and culture

homework and parent involvement with homework vary greatly across the globe enables school leaders to recognize challenges and provide the support needed for students and parents to fully participate in American schooling. Knowledge that homework expectations are not universal will help school leaders consider the best ways to share local expectations or practices and the rationale for them.

Another area where cultural experiences abroad influence parents' views about American schools is centered on school supplies. The expectation in most districts that families will purchase school supplies is a uniquely American phenomenon. In most western countries children are expected to bring very little with them to school, perhaps just a small number of pencils in a pencil case. The school purchases and distributes books, paper, markers, notebooks, crayons, manipulatives, calculators, and so on. The school requesting that students supply trade books, notebooks, crayons, tissues, wipes, printer paper, paper towels, calculators, and more seems quite strange to many parents who were educated abroad and can make them wonder if the school is effectively administered and prepared to teach lessons. Finally, when parents have limited resources and they purchase the requested supplies and then they are not used by their child to complete schoolwork, this too seems odd to many foreign-born parents (and American-born parents, too). Contact with the school is one of the major ways families are integrated into American society. Parents' impressions of interactions with the school influence their positive and negative impressions of American opportunities and weaknesses. Forward-thinking school leaders may even create a glossary of American school terms (bus note, early dismissal, superintendent's hearing, honor roll, etc.) as these may not have direct translations into parents' native language or cultural reference points.

It is critical for school administrators to become aware of international school practices. If one notices that there are a large number of students from a particular region or regions in your school, it would be critically helpful to become familiar with schooling in those countries (Rong & Preissle, 2009). Perhaps a staff development trip to that country to visit schools and government education officials to learn more about the practices, policies, and expectations in place would be possible and certainly beneficial. If a study trip is not possible, perhaps one might reach out to the embassy delegations and ask them if they could present a workshop about schools in their country to the faculty. Embassy delegations are here to support the needs of their citizens while those citizens are in the United States, and supporting education certainly fits into the delegations' mandates. *Educating*

Immigrant Students in the 21st Century: What Educators Need to Know by Rong and Preissle (2009) provides descriptions of educational systems on each continent. Reading about various regional and national philosophical orientations, pedagogy, and educational structures will help American school administrators respond more effectively to the needs of culturally and linguistically diverse students and parents who are immigrants, children of immigrants, and American-born citizens.

Promote Communication Practices

Communication is a central point of focus when trying to change school culture. Teachers, student teachers, university faculty, and administrators need to be aware of the work that is being done on behalf of the students. Students need to celebrate achievement too. Sustaining change and a culture that works requires many channels of communication, especially in the changing suburbs, because the range of partners will include those who have been educated abroad and may have limited English skills. Therefore, communication should be oral, digital, visual, and in print. As the educational background of the parents may vary significantly (from parents who are illiterate in their native language to parents who have earned graduate degrees in their countries), using a wide range of media will assure open avenues for dialogue (Rong & Preissle, 2009). Communication should support the languages spoken in the school in a balanced and respectful manner.

Assess Climate and Culture

Engaged administrators can assess the school climate and culture through journaling, designing feedback surveys (oral and written), tracking attendance of students for school days and parents at school events, and using other assessment techniques as well. Interestingly, high rates of attendance have been linked in research to positive school climate. Culture is often harder to assess. Surveys and one-to-one conversations may help educators assess school culture. One-to-one contact with constituents and stakeholders is especially important in collecting data about culture and climate in the changing suburbs in order to bridge cultural and linguistic divides. Action research with an ethnographic focus may also support educators in understanding the cultural workings of their schools. Other techniques for assessing climate and culture can be drawn from best practices in school administration such as focus groups, walk-throughs, document analyses, leadership maps, climate checklists, cultural environment rating scales, and classroom or event observations. Administrators should try to triangulate (use at least three different techniques) to assure that they are able to develop the most accurate and helpful assessment of school climate and culture.

Concluding Remarks

Celebrating success is absolutely central to making sustainable change. The culturally focused processes of supporting educators, students, and families in changing suburban schools discussed in this chapter allow school leaders to assure high-quality schooling for students in the changing suburbs. Bringing together diverse cultural resources to assure that the changing school community is supportive of all is a challenge but worth the effort. Through care, openness, and thoughtfulness, school leaders can open up a world of opportunities for students and their families.

4

Professional Development

Kristin's heart sank as she read the handwritten poster hanging in the ladies' restroom off of the main lobby of Sunnyside School: It is low class to throw trash on the floor. Kristin wondered how someone could be so callous with one's choice of words, especially in a school that served predominantly working-class poor families. This was her introduction to the school, and unfortunately it was a first of many instances that highlighted a gross misunderstanding of the families and the community surrounding the school. As a consultant hired to work with teachers on their literacy teaching and learning, Kristin quickly realized that this is where the group's work had to begin.

School leaders have been faced with increasingly complex challenges, including increased accountability, shifting demographics, and standards-based reform. In order to meet these complex challenges, school and district leaders are looking for new ways to improve student achievement and support teacher growth. Practices of the past are no longer meeting the complex demands faced in schools.

Customarily, professional development has occurred outside the school context. Teachers have left their schools and classrooms to engage in daylong workshops provided by an expert. Despite everyone's best intentions, these workshops have not had an impact on classroom practices or on student learning. In most cases, the information presented is detached from individual teachers' everyday realities and rarely involves follow-up in classrooms. As a result, teachers do not actually integrate the information or practices presented into their individual classrooms (Sykes, 1996; Willis, 2002). School leaders can no longer rely on these outdated practices but rather must reframe schools as learning centers that support the continual growth and learning of all the members of the school community.

This chapter presents research on the characteristics of high-quality professional development and the role of the school leader in the professional learning of teachers. Examples are provided from the field about successful professional initiatives in changing suburban schools.

Characteristics of High-Quality Professional Development

The ultimate goal of professional development is student achievement. With this goal at the center, research has clearly shown that in order to be effective, professional learning must honor teachers' experiences and acknowledge teachers' beliefs, build trust, be collaborative and relevant to teachers' needs, focus on student achievement, and be adequately funded.

Honors Teachers' Experiences and Acknowledges Teachers' Beliefs

Professional development has traditionally been framed as something that is *done to* teachers. Recently, policymakers and leaders have come face-to-face with the challenges that exist in schools and have forced teachers to learn new programs and follow the same script. However, such a stance on how to best help teachers needs to shift from professional development as training done to others, to *professional learning with* teachers. In this framework for professional learning, adult learning theory must be considered (Kegan, 2000; Speck, 1996). Adult learners come to learning with diverse experiences, knowledge, interests, and abilities. Adult-learner characteristics and beliefs need to be taken into account when planning learning experiences. The following exercise can be used to get to know teachers.

1. Make a three-column chart.

2. In the first column, quickly write down a list of all of the teachers with whom you are working.

3. In the second column, next to each teacher's name, write one thing that is unique about that individual in school.

4. In the last column, write one unique thing about that teacher's life outside of school.

Builds Trust

Building, growing, and maintaining trust is imperative in communities that foster professional learning. It is important for teachers to trust their leaders and trust each other to be able to take risks, ask questions, and engage fully in learning experiences that challenge beliefs. The exercise in the previous section helps leaders get to know their teachers as individuals, both inside and outside of school, and use that knowledge to build trust. In order for leaders to gain the trust of teachers, they have to first begin to trust others (teachers, students, and families) and use them as valuable resources in the school. In other words, school leaders need to share power. School leaders do this by using more inclusive language (we, us, our), and by expressing hopes and beliefs about the professional learning of the community.

As leaders of professional learning, school leaders must also take the stance of the learner. We have all been to workshops where the principals or school leaders introduce the speaker and then, after a half hour or so, head back to their office because they have work to do. Teachers' time is equally valuable, and everyone in a school community has work to do. School leaders who design experiences that they expect their teachers to engage in fully must also engage in the learning.

Is Collaborative and Relevant

Teachers, like most individuals, are not motivated by others' goals. Keeping this in mind, school leaders and teacher educators need to ensure that they are collaboratively developing goals for professional learning *with* teachers. These goals should honor and respect teachers' experiences and build on teachers' successes, not their deficits (this sounds familiar to what we say about students).

After visiting two middle school teachers' classrooms to get to know their practices and understand the contexts in which they teach in order to better inform the professional learning experience that Kristin was asked (by the principal) to lead, Kristin noticed a few common threads as possible starting places for their work together as a group. First, the teachers were all conferring with students, but the conferences included only the students reporting the title, author, and short summary of the book they were reading; no teaching was taking place during the conference. Second, the classrooms were dominated by teacher talk; students talked only when a question was directly asked by the teacher.

Before meeting as a group, Kristin sent the teachers an e-mail message to thank them for opening up their classrooms; she also communicated their strengths as teachers and named one strength that she saw in each teacher's practices (for example, the classroom was managed well). Kristin ended the e-mail by stating that she looked forward to working together at their next meeting. Then, based on the common needs that Kristin saw in each classroom, she prepared a two-hour study group on a reading workshop with a special focus on conferring.

Kristin began the study group by thanking the teachers again and reiterating the positive practices that she had witnessed in each of their classrooms. Kristin then moved to the common themes that had been observed as potential places to begin together, with the chosen topic of conferring. As she spoke, Kristin could sense the tension growing in the room (in previous learning experiences with this team, she knew that they consistently questioned new practices and pushed back against the presenters), but she continued by handing out a short reading for each of them to read to begin their conversation. After reading the piece, one of the teachers verbally expressed her strong concerns and immense dissatisfaction with the topic that had been chosen to start their work together.

While reflecting back on this experience (which has both strengths and weaknesses in its design), Kristin realized that, first and foremost, the principal had asked the group to work together based on practices that she perceived as needing improvement. Second, although Kristin had spent time in each classroom to better understand the classroom realities each teacher faced and the literacy practices they believed in, the teachers and Kristin had very different perspectives on where to start the professional learning. Kristin had started with a perceived deficit, one which *she* thought needed to be addressed and a goal that *she* believed was relevant to these teachers' needs rather than what they believed to be important.

Focused on Student Achievement

Investing in teachers will in turn result in student learning that will be demonstrated by better student performance on standardized tests. Numerous studies have reported that increased professional knowledge leads to improved student performance (Allington, 2006; National Commission on Teaching and America's Future, 1996, 1997), and federal policies have focused squarely on both high-quality teachers and improved student performance. One cannot argue that professional learning has occurred with the goal of improved student learning. However, improved student performance was mostly assumed and often ill defined.

In these increasingly complex times, with added emphasis on data-driven results, it is no longer acceptable to assume that the investment in teacher learning is making a difference for students. School leaders now must define for themselves what is meant by improved student learning, hold themselves accountable for the investment they make in teacher learning, and ensure that this investment results in improved student performance.

Adequately Funded

School leaders have to make difficult decisions about priorities and their shrinking budgets. In a recent study on professional development spending in four districts, Miles and Hornbeck (2000) found that districts spent between 2.4 and 5.9 percent of the operating budget on professional development (a sum ranging from $2,010 to $6,628 per teacher). School leaders are urged to use their professional development dollars on practices that are both research based and cost effective.

Contexts, Strategies, and Structures for Professional Learning

Adult learning theory also teaches us that we must provide varied professional learning opportunities that challenge and support individual teachers (Drago-Severson, 2004). There are many contexts, strategies, and structures for professional learning to meet the needs of teachers, support students' learning goals, and align with research-defined characteristics of high-quality professional learning.

School-Based Professional Development

A school's staff can and should take ownership and responsibility for their own professional learning goals and design. One example comes from a group of second grade teachers who had an informal discussion at lunch about an article on the importance of having multicultural literature in classroom libraries. They decided that they wanted to analyze their own classroom libraries for multicultural literature. Together, they sat in each other's classrooms and studied the books. They realized that, while they had focused previously on leveling their classroom libraries to match students' reading levels, they now also needed to include books that mirrored their changing student population. Their students needed to read books that allowed them to see themselves reflected in the characters and experiences so that they could feel valued as members of the classroom and the larger society (Bishop, 1990; Gangi, 2008). The teachers identified resources for multicultural literature that would be appropriate for their classroom libraries and began to rebuild them. These teachers found that their students began to speak more excitedly about the characters in their books.

School–University Partnership as a Structure for Professional Learning

Collaborations between schools and universities offer extensive possibilities for professional learning for every educator who is involved. Chapter 6 is dedicated to school–university partnerships and details the various ways in which these partnerships can support professional learning. Returning to the vignette at the beginning of the chapter, Kristin, as a university consultant, realized that many of the teachers at the school had never walked around the community. Some of them admitted that they were scared to do so, and some had never even thought about doing it. Kristin and the teachers launched a small miniethnography research project. First, they unpacked some of their hidden assumptions about the community (and therefore the families that lived and worked in it). By getting these assumptions out on the table, they were able to begin to deconstruct them and begin to collect data to support or discredit their claims.

Some of the assumptions that the teachers held about the community and the families were

- the neighborhood is dangerous,
- the families do not care about education (they never show up to meetings; homework is not done, done poorly, or never checked),
- there are no books in the homes, and
- parents (if even present in the household) cannot read.

Curt Dudley-Marling (2007) wrote about the return of the deficit view: that students from low-income or minority families are believed to have limited experiences, language, and culture. Many of the teachers held a deficit view of the students, families, and the neighborhood. As a consequence of these deficit views, many of the students in their classroom were initially identified as at risk, below grade level, and in need of remediation. These deficiencies were seen as something to be remediated by learning accurate cultural and linguistic (or white middle class) practices valued in schools (which for many students meant abandoning their language and culture of the families and communities). In contrast, linguistic research has shown the richness and complexity of language used by children and families living in poverty (Gee, 2004; Heath, 1983; Labov 1972).

Guided by an exercise in *Girls, Social Class, and Literacy: What Teachers Can Do to Make a Difference* (Jones, 2006) and a resource on community mapping (Treadway, 2000), Kristin and the teachers used observations, participant observations, interviews, informal discussions, photography, field notes, and documents from local newspapers and flyers to collect data and record and analyze their experiences.

Below are some of the questions and inquiries that were used:

- What organizations exist in the community (churches, businesses, etc.)?
- Describe the geography and architecture of the community.
- What style of housing is available?
- What do families do for recreation?
- Where do families feel most comfortable and why? Where do families feel least comfortable and why?
- What are the various kinds of employment available in the area (domestic, government, industry, construction, etc.)?
- Describe the employment of various family members.

Together they spent a year in the community and back at the school gathering and analyzing data in relation to the implications for teaching and learning. They also did a lot of reading to better understand the cultural and cognitive resources that their students brought to the classroom (Moll, Amanti, Neff, & Gonzalez, 1992). This school–university professional learning experience enabled this group of teachers to work together to change their thinking about the families that were part of their school community and reframe their teaching practices based on the strengths of the families and community.

Analyzing Student Work

Professional learning that is centered on the development, collection, and analysis of assessments allows teachers to learn about their students' strengths and needs; design individual, small-group, and whole-class teaching that is responsive to students' needs; and deepen their knowledge of their curriculum.

The fourth grade team at Jefferson Elementary School in New Rochelle, New York, decided that they needed to design a writing-performance assessment to start their yearlong inquiry of teaching and learning within a writing-workshop framework. Their intent in doing so was based on their need to

- get to know the students as writers,
- provide a place to start their teaching, and
- collect data to monitor student growth in writing.

They developed an assessment that included a writing prompt and revised the holistic scoring rubric (connected to New York state standards and assessments) that they used to score the writing. After giving the assessment, the teachers individually read each of their students' writing, completed a T-chart of the student's strengths and weaknesses, and used the rubric to score student work. They also exchanged their students' writing so that a second reader could comment and score the assessments. They then discussed any questions that had arisen about scoring and expectations. These conversations helped the teachers create shared goals for their students, develop a common language about the essentials of writing workshop for their students, and determine patterns and trends that needed to be addressed across the grade level.

The teachers began by developing a unit of study on narrative writing that included both minilessons related to the genre and minilessons connected to students' needs. Then, teachers worked individually and in pairs to develop minilessons that could be used for the whole class and in small groups. Teachers also role-played various possibilities for conferring with students one-to-one or in partnerships.

Teachers met together on a weekly basis to reflect on their teaching, discuss students' work, and develop minilessons and new units. At the end of each unit, teachers used the writing rubric that they had developed to assess students' final writing piece and measure students' growth in writing. At the end of the year, the teachers gave the students the same writing assessment that they had taken during the first week of school to determine and compare individual growth.

This intensive, yearlong, teacher-designed professional learning experience demonstrates how analyzing student work is a form of professional learning. These teachers developed ways to better understand their students' strengths and needs, refine their teaching to meet the needs of their diverse learners, and collaborate to foster meaningful change in their classrooms for their students.

Coaching

No Child Left Behind prompted districts and schools throughout the country to move toward job-embedded professional development in the form of instructional coaching (Dole, 2004). Although coaching met the standards defined by research for high-quality professional development and was supported by many professional associations, research has not been available until recently to assess coaching's impact on teacher instruction, student achievement, and the more nuanced aspects of this emerging practice. In the past few years, however, research has been conducted and published to help us understand the roles of instructional coaches (see for example, Bean, Draper, Hall, Vandermolen, & Zigmond, 2010), the shifting and situated nature of coaching (Rainville & Jones, 2008), and coaching's positive impact on teacher instruction (Matsumura, Garnier, Correnti, Junker, & Bickel, 2010) and student achievement (Biancarosa, Bryk, & Dexter, 2010).

Coaches are in a unique position to empower teachers to become leaders and sources of support for others. By capitalizing on the strengths of their colleagues and working toward the goal of empowerment, coaches can create powerful professional communities committed to sustained change.

There is no one model or process of coaching that can be expected to occur; rather, the process of coaching will unfold differently in each context and situation (Bean et al., 2010; Rainville & Jones, 2008). Even when coaches receive similar preparation for the position, coaching will look different in each school and in each classroom (Rainville & Jones, 2008).

Coaches can use various methods to meet teachers' individual needs for professional learning. Figure 4.1 provides a small sample of possible methods coaches can use to facilitate professional learning.

Mentoring Programs

Mentoring has tremendous value in supporting the professional learning of new teachers and new school and district administrators. Mentoring relationships provide a safe context for dialogue, reflective

Figure 4.1   Select Sample of Coaching Methods

One-to-One	Small Teams	Whole School/ Districtwide
• Educational discussions • Demonstration lessons • Collaborative lessons • Coaching visits • Examining student work • Classroom environment • Student assessments	• Examining student work • Curriculum mapping • Curriculum planning • Reading and discussing research • Investigating practices • Unpacking data • Linking data to classroom practices	• Introducing new practices • Creating a common vision, language, or set of goals • Facilitating instructional meetings

practice, examining practices and beliefs, and risk taking (Danielson, 1999; Killion, 2000; Moir & Bloom, 2003). Traditionally, mentoring relationships in schools have been associated with teacher induction programs. However, many would argue that mentoring has grown beyond supporting new educators and that all of us need a variety of mentors throughout our lives as we approach new challenges both personally and professionally. Mentors use many of the strategies that coaches employ; however, mentoring is predominantly focused on new educators and those moving into new roles to help support the mentee with the nuances of a new position.

Mentoring is a reciprocal relationship that provides both the mentor and the mentee with experiences for personal or professional reflection, learning, and growth. Research has identified several factors for mentoring to be effective. First, mentors need support in developing techniques that have proven to be successful, such as listening and communication skills, providing ongoing support, and establishing trust (Danielson, 1999; Killion, 2000; Moir & Bloom, 2003). Next, mentors should have knowledge of adult learning to best offer support and strategies (Daresh, 2003; Moir & Bloom, 2003). Lastly, mentors should be skilled at providing opportunities for instructional support and growth through strategies such as discussions, classroom visitations, demonstration lessons, and coteaching (Moir & Bloom, 2003; Rowley, 1999).

Informally, new teachers and administrators have shared that mentoring relationships have provided them with a trusted advisor to help them navigate their new positions (from simple tasks such as taking attendance electronically to more complex tasks such as handling emergency situations with the public). Given the research that exists about the value of mentoring as a strategy for helping with professional learning and growth, school leaders should find ways to develop strong mentoring programs in their districts for those in new positions.

School Visitations

Teaching can be an isolating profession. In a collaborative and trusting school community, where everyone is positioned as a learner, school visitations empower teachers to open up their classrooms to other teachers inside (intravisitations) and outside (intervisitations) their school.

Intraschool visitations. Teachers often hear about engaging lessons happening in other classrooms but rarely get to see these activities in action. Instead, teachers share their own perspective on how they planned and executed such lessons and how the lessons went. Schools that value professional learning invite teachers to visit each other's classrooms. School leaders can support teachers by working alongside them to collaboratively plan intraschool classroom visits and can use these visitations as the impetus for helping teachers talk about and refine their teaching practices.

Interschool or district visitations. Videos provide a glimpse of other teachers in action, but often times these videos seem to be staged or are occurring in classrooms that do not mirror the diverse classrooms in which teachers work. For example, teachers can see bits and pieces of a reading workshop on a video; however, to see the entire workshop orchestrated with the realities that teachers face (e.g., constant interruptions, independent reading while meeting with small groups, and students' handling of the materials) is powerful. This is especially important for those who are doubters or cannot visualize how twenty-five students can all be reading different books. Instead of, or in addition to videos, teachers can visit classrooms in other schools and districts with similar communities that are successfully implementing strategies that they need to learn more about or adopt. In addition to the actual classroom visit, time should be allocated to meet with the teacher for a debriefing session after the visit. Debriefing sessions provide a valuable opportunity to learn from colleagues about their experiences, successes, and struggles.

As the Changing Suburbs Institute has grown, newer professional development schools (PDSs) have brought groups of teachers to visit PDSs that have been long-standing partners with Manhattanville

College. During their visit, they meet with the administration to discuss the role of the principal in the PDS and learn about the evolution of the PDS from the leader's perspective. The team then meets with the school's PDS leadership team to learn about the structure of the team and the role it plays in leading and supporting the PDS's initiatives. The team then visits various classrooms that have direct connections with PDS's projects, for example, field-based classes, small-group tutoring sessions, or cotaught lessons. These visits offer a glimpse into potential possibilities for the partnership and help teachers to begin thinking about how the partnership can best be shaped to meet the needs of their classrooms and school. See Box 4.1 for guidelines for planning a classroom or school visit.

Box 4.1   Guidelines for Planning a Classroom or School Visit

The following recommendations help to plan successful classroom or school visits:

- Plan ahead. Goals for the visit should be discussed. Provide time for a previsit conference to help set the purpose for the visit and give the teachers an opportunity to introduce their context and discuss a rationale for the visit.
- Make sure that teachers are prepared.
  - *Visiting teachers* should be informed about the classroom or school's community, vision, and approach to student learning. Provide teachers with instructions or prompts, for example, specific practices to pay attention to or whether to ask questions during the classroom visit or the debriefing session.
  - *Host teachers* should be informed about the purpose of the visit, the number of teachers to expect, and the schedule for the day.
- Allow sufficient time for the visit to take place. Use university interns, student teachers, or substitute teachers to provide coverage for the visiting teacher.
- Provide time for teachers to debrief. Teachers will want to discuss questions and concerns that arose during the visit. The host teacher may want to discuss adaptations and modifications that occurred during teaching in response to student needs.
- Provide time for teachers to determine the next steps for their learning, which might include another visit, coteaching, a planning meeting, or just time for the visiting teacher to explore the practice in his or her own classroom.

Action Research

Educators often use action research as a tool to help them systematically investigate a question, problem, or issue that has arisen in

---

Box 4.2   From the Assistant Professor's Desk on Action Research

Ross Collin, Assistant Professor of Literacy at Manhattanville College, recently facilitated an action-research group at a local middle school. The teacher–researchers in the group represented a range of content areas, from science to physical education. Teacher–researchers began their work by identifying and discussing pedagogical questions that arose from their teaching. Ross set parameters around this discussion by stipulating that the questions should have some bearing on student achievement. A science teacher spoke up in the discussion and said that she was not satisfied with the ways she grouped students in her classes. Over the next two sessions, she turned this thought into an action-research question by speaking with her colleagues in the action-research group and consulting professional literature. At this step, Ross helped the teacher find relevant literature that could ground the question at the center of her project. Initially, her central question was What are the most pedagogically sound ways of breaking up classes into small groups? Having formed her question, she worked to develop new ways of grouping her students and sought to devise ways of measuring the effects of her interventions. To gather information at this stage, she read professional literature, met with Ross, spoke with her own colleagues in the group and across the school, and surveyed her students. Reflecting on what she learned at this stage, she realized that she should revise her central question to read How can teachers engage students in devising small groups appropriate for specific classes? She then went back through the literature and had additional discussions with Ross, her students, and her colleagues. She then created ways of negotiating grouping rules with different classes of students. Once comfortable with the information that she had gathered and the decisions that she had made, she tried out her intervention plan in her classes and gathered data on students' experiences and learning. She took notes on students' work, compared their quiz scores with their scores from earlier in the year, and surveyed students to gather their thoughts on the new grouping rules. Ultimately, through debriefing discussions with Ross and other teachers in the research group, she concluded that it was best to switch throughout the year between teacher-selected and teacher-and-student-selected small groups. At a faculty assembly at the end of the year, she presented her findings to her colleagues and strengthened the school's understanding of group work.

their practice. The goal of action research is the improvement of teaching and learning in classrooms and schools. The example in Box 4.2 explains how one middle school teacher used action research to help her determine how to group her students for science instruction.

The Role of the School Leader in the Professional Development of Teachers

School leaders are at the heart of professional learning. They are responsible for establishing the conditions for others to succeed, monitoring progress toward the goal, and keeping people motivated during times of struggle.

In schools today, teachers are being bombarded with top-down initiatives. It is incredible when you see and hear experienced teachers wondering if they can do anything right. For example, in one district, each one of the curriculum areas has undergone significant changes, which means that key teachers are constantly being pulled to meet with committees to discuss curricular shifts. In addition, new assessments are being required, with the expectation that new systems are in place to collect, store, and use data. There is a push for professional learning communities (Hord, 1997) and, of course, the pressures of state testing are being felt by all. Unfortunately, this situation is common. District and school leaders are feeling tremendous pressure to raise the achievement of all of their students and in response, are adopting the newest and best practices. Workshops, instructional coaching, and professional learning communities are offered as supports for professional learning. Yet, in most cases these initiatives are occurring separately; they are not aligned, and they leave teachers overwhelmed with competing initiatives and demands on their time.

If schools are to meet the challenges of their changing student population, they must become places where adults can work and learn together to grow and change to accommodate diverse student needs.

Guidelines for School Leaders for Establishing Conditions for Successful Professional Learning

In this section, guidelines are provided to help school leaders establish a culture for professional learning in their schools.

Create a Shared Vision

Most school leaders will tell you that they have a very particular vision for where they believe their school should be headed. However, a principal's vision, on its own, is one that must be sold to faculty. In contrast, developing a shared vision based on common ideals can be an energizing learning experience that leads to program coherence and a renewed commitment to the school. Creation of this vision should include teachers' hopes and beliefs about what strong instruction and successful classrooms look and sound like. It should also challenge everyone involved to become more effective as a teacher and learner. Once this vision is clearly articulated and shared with and by everyone, various teams or committees can be formed to help make this vision a reality.

Create a Schoolwide Action Plan

Turning the school's vision into a reality can be difficult with the pop-up demands that occur in schools and school districts. The school leader should waste no time in forming a committee of administrators and teachers who will facilitate the development of the school's action plan. This committee can be called the school leadership team. An action plan is a living document that helps a

> **Guidelines for Establishing Conditions for Successful Professional Learning**
>
> - Create a shared vision
> - Create a schoolwide action plan
> - Form teams to move the plan forward
> - Articulate clearly the roles and responsibilities of coaches in promoting professional development
> - Measure impact

school carry out its vision. It is a tool that helps keep everyone on the same page and accountable for moving toward the shared goal. See Figure 4.2 for a template of an action plan framework.

Figure 4.3 is a sample of one school's initial schoolwide action plan developed by the school's leadership team. This plan was developed at the beginning of the school year after a discussion at the first faculty meeting about their current practices and beliefs about effective teaching and learning. The group did not list all assessments, and they did not define specific professional learning experiences for each teacher. The expectation is that teams will be formed to move the plan forward, and members of the leadership team will lead those smaller teams.

Form Teams to Move the Plan Forward

Once a plan is created, teams should be formed to engage everyone in moving the school action plan forward. Teaming builds individual

Figure 4.2   Schoolwide Action Plan

School: _____   Principal: _____
Coach: _____   Team Members: _____

Where are we now?	Where do we want to be by June?	What steps can we take to meet our goal?	How do we assess our progress?
• What are our beliefs about students and families? • What effective practices are currently being implemented? • What assessments are being used to drive our instruction now? • How are these assessments used and by whom?	• What are our shared beliefs about students and families? • What do we mean by effective teaching and learning? • What district initiatives must we adhere to? How do they connect to or impede with our school vision? • What is our school's goal for this year? • How can we ensure that teachers' goals align with the school's goal?	• How can we challenge our personal and shared assumptions about students and families? • What steps can we take to learn about the realities our families are living with? • What effective practices can we implement? • How will these practices support our goal? • Will these practices lead us to our goals? • What assessments can we use to drive our instruction or use as benchmark indicators? • Who will be responsible for each step?	• How can we assess our progress? • How can the coach/principal/PDS liaison support the implementation of the steps? • What is our target date for the completion of each step? • How often will this team meet? • Where will the team meet and at what time? • Who will facilitate this meeting? • Which teachers will be invited to participate?

and organizational capacity for learning through various forms of partnering and adult collaboration. Teaming also fosters collaborative cultures in which adults exchange ideas and share ownership in decision-making practices. The school leadership team can work to brainstorm a list of teams that may be necessary to move the action plan forward. For example, grade-level teams may work together to identify professional learning goals, or content-specific teams (e.g., literacy and math) can be formed to discuss and analyze schoolwide data, curriculum resources, standards, and relevant research. While the school-action plan is implemented, teams will naturally be redefined and reconfigured to meet varied professional learning needs.

Figure 4.3 Sample Schoolwide Action Plan

School: ABC Elementary School   Principal: Mrs. S. and Assistant Principal Mr. P.

Coach: Ms. M. (Literacy), Mrs. S. (Math) Team Members: Ms. S. (ESL), Ms. G. (reading), Mr. A. (grade 4), Mrs. S. (grade 1), Ms. T. (social worker), Ms. P. (media specialist)

Where are we now?	Where do we want to be by June?	What steps can we take to meet our goal?	How do we assess our progress?
What are our beliefs about students and families? Currently, there is not one shared belief. As a school we try and portray a positive and inclusive attitude toward families, but this team feels that this is not how each family experiences these beliefs. There is definitely one set of parents who are actively involved and tends to be the voice of the parents. However, we have a large group of families who are not as engaged as we would like them to be. There are also faculty members who have a deficit view of families.	**What are our shared beliefs about students and families?** We would like our faculty to • Embrace and engage all parents and families as partners in learning and leading • Recognize that all families have strengths and want their children to be successful both in and out of school	**How can we challenge our personal and shared assumptions about students and families?** • Shared readings and discussions about cultural/linguistic/economic differences and culturally relevant pedagogy • Investigations into our community • Parents educate faculty and administration about their realities	**How can we assess our progress?** • Coaches will be in classrooms to support teachers as they shift practices • Administration will conduct walk-throughs looking for signs of movement toward the goals • Teacher evaluations and observations will include discussions about individual teacher's goals, movement toward those goals, and how they connect to school goals • Design ways to assess professional learning (interviews, surveys, walk-throughs)
What effective practices are currently being implemented? There are many effective practices being used, but they are not consistent across all grade levels and subject areas. *Literacy:* • Small-group instruction, identified as guided reading; however, use and implementation is not consistent (e.g., not a consistent understanding of guided reading).	**What do we mean by effective teaching and learning?** Effective teaching is • Driven by students' strengths and needs • Includes whole group, small group, and 1:1 instruction • Engages all children and draws on their experience • Connects to real life (skills transfer—not isolated tasks)	**What steps can we take to learn about the realities our families are living with?** • Listen to our families • Attend community events • Seek out community leaders and community partnerships • Have parents present or discuss their cultural/racial/ethnic identities **What effective practices can we implement?** • Schedule time for teacher learning as a part of their work day/week • Be explicit about coaching roles and responsibilities (literacy and math) • Differentiate our professional-learning experiences for all teachers • Have the administration engage in professional learning	**How can the coach/principal/PDS liaison support the implementation of the steps?** • Support of professional learning experiences • Constant connections to the school's goals and vision • Carefully looking at district initiatives and how they connect to school goals • Belief in teachers • Honoring teachers' experiences and beliefs • Recognize that change is hard
	What district initiatives must we adhere to? How do they connect to or impede with our school vision? The district wants us to begin to use • Common Core State Standards • AIMSweb for progress monitoring		

(Continued)

79

Figure 4.3   (Continued)

Where are we now?	Where do we want to be by June?	What steps can we take to meet our goal?	How do we assess our progress?
• Teachers have a basic understanding of balanced literacy practices and are using many aspects of balanced literacy in their classrooms (independent reading, teacher modeling, readers' notebooks). Use and understanding of practices is inconsistent. • All teachers integrate technology into their classroom teaching. *Math:* • All teachers are using Calendar Math with consistency. • All teachers are using current curriculum materials (Investigations by TERC), though at varying levels. **What assessments are being used to drive our instruction now?** *Literacy:* • *Developmental Reading Assessment* (DRA) (Beavers, 2006) *Math:* • End of chapter tests • Teacher created assessments to varying degrees • Minute Math	• Waterford Early Learning for all children in kindergarten and grade one (computer-based reading) • Upper-grade test preparation materials (specifically Kaplan) • Teachers in grades 4–5 will be reviewed this year using New York state's new Annual Professional Performance Review system **What is our school's goal for this year?** *Literacy:* We would like to move toward a reading and writing workshop framework for curriculum and instruction within the next 3 years. In order to begin this schoolwide shift, each grade level will work to assess where they are along a continuum of learning (toward the goal) and what steps they need to take and need to be supported as a grade level and as individuals to move toward the identified goal. (Raise student achievement on state tests.) *Math:* Start to shift to the Common Core State Standards. Look critically at math curriculum and how it is meeting our students' needs and assess how we can better meet them (Pilot Singapore Math at grade 1). Make sure that we are using	**How will these practices support our goal?** • Powerful professional learning experiences will help move us toward our goals • Each grade level and individual will identify specific goals to accomplish • These goals will be shared with and supported by coaches and administration **What assessments can we use to drive our instruction or use as benchmark indicators?** • Teachers will be supported by coaches to successfully administer and use assessments to guide instruction • Teachers will use formative assessments as a part of their regular practices and keep track of these assessments	**What is our target date for the completion of each step?** • Depends on grade level and teacher goals • Will be identified at next meeting **How often will this team meet? Where will the team meet, and what time?** On the first Wednesday of each month **Who will facilitate this meeting?** We will shift so that every member facilitates one meeting **Which teachers will be invited to participate?** To keep teachers actively engaged in the process • Meeting notes will be shared with the faculty • Teacher leaders will be identified (with the goal that every teacher leads something based on his or her strengths)

How are these assessments used and by whom?
- *DRA* (Beavers, 2006) is being used twice a year by all classroom teachers. However, administration is inconsistent, and the data gathered is only being used to level children for small-group instruction that tends to be static. Data is also used to identify students who need support services.

Math:
- Assessments are mainly used as summative assessments. Need to begin shifting to formative assessment use in mathematics.

Overall State Test Scores 2010-11

Literacy:

	% below proficiency	% at proficiency
Grade 3	43	57
Grade 4	33.3	66.7
Grade 5	47.5	52.4

Math:

	% below proficiency	% at proficiency
Grade 3	37.2	62.7
Grade 4	37.8	62.2
Grade 5	28.9	71

assessments to guide our instruction and monitor progress. Provide more consistent math support to students who have been identified as needing intervention. (Raise student achievement on state tests.)

How can we ensure that teachers' goals align with the school's goal?
Build structures that support teacher learning, teacher conversations, and talk. Goals include
- Consistent grade-level meetings (with and without coaching)
- Job-embedded professional development (in classroom coaching cycles)
- Intra- and interclassroom and school visits
- Build teacher leaders on different topics

Who will be responsible for each step?
- Literacy and math coaches will work alongside each grade level and individual to help identify goals and create a plan for their work together
- Based on identified goals, coaches will create a schedule for working with teachers
- Goals will be shared with faculty and administration to help support each other
- Coaches will use planning documents (e.g., teacher contact forms, weekly calendars, monthly summaries, demonstration lesson response forms) to guide and keep track of their work

Source: Adapted from work by Janice McDowell and Matthew Hall.

Figure 4.4   Coaching Program Handout From Lakewood Public Schools

Coach Responsibilities

- Make ongoing classroom visitations as appropriate and necessary to be able to perform the duties of literacy and math coach.

Essential Criteria

- Develop a schedule that is appropriate and equitable to teachers within the school.
- Keep abreast of current research-based practices.
- Maintain the confidentiality of teachers and classrooms.
- Hold high expectations for teachers (and other professionals) as well as their students.
- Model the characteristics of a reflective professional who monitors and evaluates one's own professional activities with the goal of continual growth and development.
- Work in partnership to improve schoolwide literacy and math goals.

- Provide content knowledge and resources about learning and teaching literacy and math.

Essential Criteria

- Develop and participate in professional development activities to build capacity as a resource for the school and to model professional behavior.
- Prepare materials for the use of the Lakewood Public Schools and teachers including teaching strategies, assessment techniques, assessment of reading and math skills, interpretation of assessment results, classroom routines, and practices that promote literacy and math.

- Provide information and guidance regarding a range of effective and innovative literacy and math practices to teachers and administrators.

Essential Criteria. Utilize various avenues such as:

- Individual discussions (informal or formal)
- Demonstrations lesson *with pre- and postdiscussion analysis*
- Study groups
- Professional development and/or inservice training programs
- Workshops

- Assist building and classroom-level educators in implementing challenging and rigorous curriculum based on the New Jersey Core Content Curriculum Standards (NJCCCS).

Essential Criteria

- Develop and participate in professional development activities to build capacity as a resource for schools and to model professional behavior.
- Model lessons in accordance with NJCCCS and make this explicit.

- Record and disseminate information on coaching work.

Essential Criteria

- Write work summaries in such a manner as to provide teacher confidentiality.
- Provide building principals, supervisors, and Assistant Superintendent of Curriculum with copies of summaries.
- Meet with building principals, supervisors, and Assistant Superintendent of Curriculum to discuss content of summaries as requested.

Articulate Clearly the Roles and Responsibilities of Coaches in Promoting Professional Development

Despite the growing number of coaching positions in schools, the roles and responsibilities of coaches are vaguely defined and can lead to confusion and stalled initiatives. In order to support and sustain change, the roles and responsibilities of the coach should be articulated and shared widely. Figure 4.4 offers ideas for coaching expectations that were created by coaches and school district leaders in a New Jersey school district for literacy and math coaches. The principal gave this handout to teachers to help them better understand what coaches would be able to do for them and their classrooms. When school leaders clarify a coach's role, the coach is better able to focus on helping teachers accomplish the schoolwide action plan.

Measure Impact

The goal of professional learning is twofold: shift teacher beliefs and practices and improve student learning. Traditionally, professional learning evaluations have included teachers' feelings about their experiences (and often include statements that do not reflect learning or future shifts in teaching that may occur). School leaders and their teams can determine the impact of professional learning experiences on teacher and student learning by designing a process to collect qualitative and quantitative data in relation to the defined goals. This process is most effective before the professional learning process takes place to ensure that student and teacher pre- and postdata can be collected. Data sources can include observations of teachers' changes in student engagement and the depth of student understanding and teacher surveys or interviews that include reflections about their learning experiences and how it shifted their teaching practices.

Concluding Remarks

We know a lot about professional learning. We know that it is essential for lasting school improvement. We know the contexts of professional learning experiences that lead to improved teaching practices. We know that the investment in professional learning is a high-leverage investment because it has the potential to raise student achievement for even the most marginalized students. Despite all that we know about the potential of professional learning, we have continued to spin our wheels and allow others to define what is important for us. It is time for schools and school leaders to chart their own course for professional learning.

5

Implementing Programs for Culturally and Linguistically Diverse Student Populations

Imagine that you are a ten-year-old American girl who loves school. Your native language is English, and it is the only language you speak. You get good grades in school and have an active extracurricular and social life that includes a wide circle of friends, sports, and dance. Life is good. At dinner one night, Dad announces that he has a new job opportunity, and your family is moving to Saudi Arabia.

Fast-forward to your first day of school in Saudi Arabia. Dad escorts you to your new school. On your way to school, Dad advises you to not look around and, in particular, not to look at men. You find this strange, but you are more concerned and nervous about being in a new school and fitting into the new class. And you are physically uncomfortable. The required headdress and long-sleeved dress are too hot for the climate, and you cannot move around easily. You feel very confined. Once in the classroom you check out your surroundings. The desks are all stationary. The classroom walls are bare. On the chalkboard there are markings that look like pretty designs, along with some drawings that look like the sun and its rays and a flower and its leaves. All the other students are female; no males in sight. The teacher standing in the front is a woman also dressed in loose-fitting clothing that covers her body completely, except for her hands. She is wearing a headdress, and her face is covered with a veil so that all you can see are her beautiful dark eyes. The headdresses remind you of what Whoopi Goldberg wore in the movie Sister Act.

The teacher is in the front of the room gesturing to the chalkboard and speaking to you in Arabic and, despite the couple of classes your family took before moving to Saudi Arabia, you do not understand. You can't make any sense of it. She is writing squiggles from right to left as she is speaking. She points toward you and says something. You do not respond because you do not have a clue as to what she is saying. The teacher continues to speak in your direction, raising her voice louder and louder. She seems to be angry. A classmate next to you motions for you to stand up. Perplexed, you stand up, look the teacher in the eyes, and say in English, "I don't know what you want me to do!"

The above scenario is an adaptation from Denise McKeon's (2004) *When Meeting "Common" Standards Is Uncommonly Difficult* to illustrate the dynamics that come into play when students negotiate language, content, and cultural customs. It is a common scene that occurs in schools throughout the nation that are experiencing a change in their student population. The lesson in the vignette was about photosynthesis, a concept our American student understood. However, cultural and linguistic differences prohibited the student from understanding what the teacher was saying and what she wanted the American student to do. The teacher's perceived anger was a result of the girl not following the customs of the Middle Eastern culture (students stand to respond to the teacher) and her inability to express her knowledge in the language of the classroom.

This chapter discusses what school leaders need to know for identifying, implementing, and assessing programs to meet the needs of diverse student populations. With a focus on the school and classroom context, general intervention ideas and specific program descriptions are presented for creating K–12 culturally responsive classrooms.

Overview of Program Needs for Diverse Student Populations

Challenges

Diversity is often discussed through the analogy of weaving a beautiful tapestry. Maya Angelou's (1993) memoir speaks about equality and race. "We all should know that diversity makes for a rich tapestry, and we must understand that all the threads of the tapestry are equal in value no matter what their color" (p. 124). Her view blends together some of the primary dimensions of diversity, or *otherness:* race, ethnicity, age, gender, physical qualities, and sexual orientation (University of Maryland, 2005). Schools, however, must address not only the primary dimensions of diversity in their schools' populations but also some of the secondary factors of diversity: educational background, income status, religious beliefs, and life experiences (University of Maryland, 2005).

The challenges are many with regard to providing quality education for many threads that create a school community. School leadership has to answer to all groups of the school district. English language learners, with their own diversity, offer an opportunity to create a new school culture encompassing all children. To achieve a culture that is rich in contrasting values, we must recognize all human potentialities to be able to weave a less arbitrary social fabric that includes all diverse human gifts (Mead, 1935).

Changing Demographics

Reportedly, approximately one in three children in our schools speaks a language other than English at home (U.S. Department of Education, National Center for Education Statistics, 2011). With suburban public schools' student population increasing to 3.4 million in the past decade and a half, almost entirely due to the enrollment of new Latino, African American, and Asian students, white suburban students have become less isolated from minority students (Fry, 2007). From 1990 to 2006, the number of Hispanic children in the nation's public schools almost doubled. U.S. census figures project that by 2050 there will be more Hispanic school-age children in our schools than non-Hispanic white students (Fry & Gonzales, 2008). Hispanics often considered as one group are in fact a very diverse group. This diversity is compounded by the rapid demographic growth of the Hispanic population, resulting in even more diversity (Suro, 2007).

In light of the changing demographics, the complexion of schools and the populations they must serve has become more and more complex and challenging. Many of the tried and true applications of instruction are no longer sufficient to educate America's children. To meet district, school, and community needs, many aspects of our educational system must be explored and evaluated.

Community Ownership/Teachers' Jobs

Paramount in dealing with the changing demographics is community ownership. Change is difficult for many groups. When a school district experiences changing demographics that result in an influx of English language learners (ELLs), the parents, teachers, administrators, and students are often fearful and suspicious of the new group. Much of this fear comes from not knowing the culture and language of the ELLs; what it means for their own families, jobs, and livelihood; and the students' needs or how to teach this new group of students.

Generally, the school community will support programs and interventions that affect their children and families in a positive way. They tend to reject ideas and programs that go against what they personally believe are necessary and important. Administrators need to cultivate a relationship with the school's community at large. One way to do this is to listen to constituents. Who are the members of the community? What does the community think the school needs? What should the administrators do if there are various community groups that disagree?

A second yet very important group whose ownership is needed to be successful is the teachers. Teachers will need to be guided and questioned regarding their philosophies and opinions about their role in providing education to ELLs. Teachers need professional development options to develop their skills in reaching the ELL student population. Including teachers in the change process can help facilitate their sense of ownership of it. Validating and accepting the teachers' ideas and concerns goes a long way toward eliminating resistance to a new program or change in the school routine. A time of change for the school is an opportunity to nurture and develop grassroots leadership of teachers. See Box 5.1 for a principal's thoughts on teacher ownership.

Competent Staff

Fundamental to serving a linguistically diverse community is employing a competent staff. Finding highly qualified teachers and

Box 5.1 From the Principal's Desk on Teacher Ownership

Principal Rosa Taylor, mentioned in Chapter 2, found that communicating the rationale behind a dual language program and providing the experience of attending conferences as a team—such as *La Cosecha* (The Harvest), New Mexico's annual dual language conference—led to both teacher buy-in and the emergence of teacher leaders. Her faculty visit schools that are implementing different models of dual language programs, participate in workshops, learn about language research, and share problems and needs of educating ELLs. The dual language teachers now advocate for their students and the program and support and mentor new teachers as they join the dual language program. One group of dual language teachers shared their experiences in a workshop on how to get started with a dual language program at a Changing Suburbs Institute (CSI) Educational Forum. This transformed them from mentees to mentors to other CSI districts.

staff to educate ELLs becomes a challenge. Qualified teachers are those who have certification to teach in their state. To teach ELLs effectively, staff need more than credentials. They need an understanding of the ELLs' culture and language. Diversity has to be embraced and celebrated. Basic knowledge of second-language acquisition and methods of teaching English as a second language contribute to teachers' success in educating ELLs.

The scope of adults who affect the educational outcomes of our students goes well beyond the teacher of the classroom. Successful schools educate the whole child. Therefore, ancillary and support staff, such as teachers' aides, school guidance counselors, and parent liaisons, also need to be committed to educating the school's diverse population. Competence becomes more a measure of flexibility and resourcefulness of the teachers and administrators.

Desired Outcomes

The major desired outcome for a changing suburban school is creation of a pluralistic and bilingual community that provides educational opportunity and access to quality education for all students. "Diversity is the one true thing we all have in common. Celebrate it every day" (Anonymous, n.d.). Diversity should be considered as an opportunity to review goals, renew faculty, and deliver a powerful and successful curriculum. English-language students contribute threads of color, texture, and variety to weave into the tapestry of a whole school community.

Helping Teachers Create Culturally Responsive Classrooms

Historically, school culture in the United States is based on the European American culture of individualistic values. For many teachers in the United States, this is how they were educated. We come to our classrooms with a set of values and expectations regarding behavior and learning of our students. As teachers, we expect our students to be polite and respectful. Respect is demonstrated by looking an adult in the eye when that adult speaks to you. Looking at someone else's paper or work is considered impolite at least and possibly cheating. In our educational system, children are generally responsible for their own learning. The remarks "keep your eyes on your own paper" and "do your own work" are often heard in our classrooms.

For much of the ELL population, school culture is not so individualistic but rather more collectivist in nature and resulting in possible cultural clashes. The behaviors that demonstrate respect can vary from culture to culture. In an adult–child relationship, Hispanic children will lower their eyes when an adult is speaking directly to them to show respect. For the U.S. culture, such behavior can be considered dismissive and disrespectful. Some cultures consider thinking and acting as an individual as taboo. The concepts of collectivism and cooperation are valued as the norm.

Assessing Culture

In an attempt to be culturally relevant, teachers often examine the culture of their students from the perspective of an outsider. This is a good beginning, but teachers must also remember that they are "people whose values and beliefs are inherently cultural" (Rothstein-Fisch & Trumbull, 2008, p. xiii).

The Bridging Cultures Project diverges from the behavioralistic model of learning by incorporating sociocultural, constructivist, and developmental viewpoints of learning. Bridging Cultures asks teachers to use the cultural framework of individualism or collectivism in order to reflect on and gain some understanding of their personal, as well as those of students and their families' cultural values. The goal is to improve their teaching and the students' learning. With the knowledge of cultural differences, teachers can become cultural brokers who look from the inside out rather than responding to the external behaviors of culturally diverse students. Fundamental to the success of teaching ELLs is making implicit cultural values explicit (Rothstein-Fisch & Trumbull, 2008).

Referring back to the vignette at the beginning of the chapter, there are many things a teacher or school leader could have done to make the cultural transition easier for the American student in the Middle East. At the school building level, there could be a Newcomer Program. This program would include all foreign-born or foreign-raised newcomers to the school. The purpose would be not only to provide linguistic support in the new language of the classroom but also to explicitly teach the culture of school in that country. Several Changing Suburbs Institute (CSI) schools have such programs. The students usually stay in the Newcomer Center for about six months. The purposeful transition to English as a second language (ESL) classes and general education classes often involve a buddy or partner who models the behavior and school culture that are expected of them in the classroom.

Valuing Diversity

Diversity is here to stay. There is a need to shift the view of diversity. Traditionally, ELL students are viewed as lacking knowledge of the English language, prerequisite literacy skills, and support from their families. This deficit view of ELLs needs to transform to one that values the diverse funds of knowledge that ELLs have. The ELL students who enter our classrooms come to us with a wealth of knowledge and traditions. Almost all ELLs enter our schools proficient and fluent in speaking and understanding orally their spoken native language. They come to us with vast and varied life experiences. Our mission is to tap into all the elements of diversity to further the education of ELLs.

The richness of diversity is an asset to a school and its community. Part of the challenge is to see each student as unique with a skill set that might not be the norm of most non-ESL students but is just as valuable. Ask the question, who are they? Culturally, there may be some common characteristics. Knowing the cultural characteristics provides a starting point for designing instruction for the student. For example, Asian ELL students tend to be less verbal and are less likely to volunteer a response in class than the average American student

(Carrasquillo & Rodriguez, 2006). With this knowledge, teachers can modify or emphasize certain parts of the curriculum to facilitate the academic progress of Asian ELLs. Looking through a lens of valuing diversity, schools can create programs and instruction that best serve ELLs and their families.

Curriculum and Program Changes

Curriculum and program changes should be initiated and implemented in response to the need or needs of the school or district and supported by data. Each district is unique, and each school in a district may be unique in its population, needs, and goals. No one magic curriculum, textbook series, or program will work for all districts. The measures and interventions taken must match the needs and staff of the school community.

CSI school districts have employed several different curriculum and program changes effectively and successfully for their particular diverse and ESL populations. In each case, the choice matched the needs of the school or district. For one CSI school principal, Eileen Santiago of Thomas A. Edison School in Port Chester, New York, the focus was to educate the whole child, which leads to the development of a full-service community school (see Chapter 7 for a full description of the school). The full-service community school forged partnerships and programs with several local agencies and organizations for medical, counseling, parent groups, and after-school enrichment (Gómez, Ferrara, Santiago, Fanelli & Taylor, 2012). For another former CSI school principal, Cynthia Slotkin, a dual language program in Italian was implemented to address the school's first- and second-generation Italian community and cultivate and maintain the Italian heritage and language.

Programs for ELLs

Most of the formal educational programs for ELLs fall under the umbrella of bilingual education. Bilingual education includes both bilingual education and teaching English to speakers of other languages (TESOL). Regardless of the type of bilingual education implemented in schools, the main objective is to become proficient in English.

Bilingual education in the United States is not a new phenomenon. The origin of bilingual education in the United States dates back to the mid-19th century (1830s) with German-English schools (Baker,

2011). Changes throughout the years relate to reasons for its use, educational and linguistic goals, processes for implementation, and related legislation.

There are several types of bilingual programs, but the two basic types are transitional and maintenance. With basic assimilation as its primary goal, the transitional program moves the child from his or her home language, the minority language, to the majority language of school instruction, in our case English. Monolingualism is the objective. There are two types of transitional programs: early exit and late exit. The early exit transitional bilingual education usually provides native-language support for a maximum of two years, while the late exit continues native-language support for approximately 40 percent of classroom instruction until the sixth grade. The transitional process does not necessarily lead to a bilingual child. Some students lose the ability to communicate proficiently in the home language. In some cases, students of transitional programs experience loss of their home language (Wong-Fillmore, 1991). The goal of both maintenance varieties of bilingual education is to maintain or develop and maintain the student's native language. The maintenance varieties foster and develop the student's cultural identity, leading to cultural pluralism. The developmental maintenance programs seek equal proficiency and biliteracy in the home language and English (Baker, 2011).

Dual Language

Currently, one of the most effective and popular forms of bilingual education is the dual language (DL) program. "Dual language education is the curricular mainstream, taught through two languages. Students are educated together throughout the day in cognitively challenging, grade-level academic content in interactive classes" (Collier & Thomas, 2009, p. 66). Under the umbrella of maintenance and developmental bilingual education, the DL approach delivers grade-level curriculum in both language minority and language majority. Students are learning the content material in both the native and second language and, at the same time, developing both home-language and second-language proficiency. The notion of curriculum or services being "taken away" from a group of children, as mentioned in Chapter 1, is eliminated. In fact, white parents view DL programs as value-added during these times of severe budgetary cuts. The impetus for one CSI school to investigate the idea of a DL program and eventually implement one came from a comment from a white parent during a school meeting. The father stated that ELL students come into the school speaking one language and leave speaking two. He wanted his children to have the same opportunity to become bilingual. Likewise, there are parents who are recent immigrants or are first- and second-generation immigrants who want their children to preserve and develop their native language. In a recent edition of *Siempre Mujer,* a Spanish-language women's magazine similar to *Family Circle,* an article titled "ABCD . . . >¡*Español!*>" states, "*Uno de los mayors desafíos de las madres hispanas en Estados Unidos es que sus hijos conserven el idioma de sus raíces>*" (One of the greatest challenges of Hispanic mothers in the United States is that their children maintain the language of their roots) (Cabrera, 2011, p. 94).

There are two basic models of dual language: two-way and one-way programs. Both types can be either 90:10 or 50:50. The basic difference between a two-way and a one-way program is demographics. In the one-way model, there are two languages being used to teach the curriculum, but the student population represents one language group. For those communities that have basically a homogeneous language group of ELLs, the one-way model of bilingual education is often employed. Several school districts in Texas, where the student population is overwhelmingly Spanish-speaking ELLs, are adopting the Gomez and Gomez one-way enrichment model because the demographics of the area do not represent two language groups (Estrada, Gómez, & Ruiz-Escalante, 2009). Two-way dual language programs teach content through two languages to two language groups of students. The two-way model helps foster access and equity for all students in the school (Calderón & Minaya-Rowe, 2003).

The ratios 90:10 and 50:50 refer to the relationship of instructional time taught in the native (minority) language and the target (majority) language. In the beginning of the 90:10 model, there is an emphasis in the minority language. For example, if English is the basic school language of instruction (majority language) and Spanish is the native language of the ELL (minority language), 90 percent of instruction in pre-K through first grade is in Spanish and the remaining 10 percent is in English. Each year, as the students progress though the program, the percentages shift with instruction in the majority language, until the percentages are equal in the fourth or fifth grade (Grade 2: 80% Spanish, 20% English; Grade 3: 70% Spanish, 30% English; Grade 4: 60% Spanish, 40% English; Grade 5: 50% Spanish, 50% English). At the middle and high school levels, the students continue to be instructed in both languages. The 50:50 model is similar to the 90:10 model except there is no graduated instruction between the two languages. Continuing with the example of English being the majority language and Spanish the minority, in the 50:50 model, curriculum is presented and instructed 50 percent of the time in Spanish and 50 percent of the time in English at the start of pre-K or kindergarten (Collier & Thomas, 2009). The percentages remain at 50:50 through twelfth grade.

Dual language programs are appealing to school districts for several reasons. Two positive results of DL programs are that they "promote bilingualism, respect, and equity for all students in a school" (Calderon & Minaya-Rowe, 2003, p. xi) and improve student achievement. Collier and Thomas's (2009) longitudinal studies of DL programs in a variety of languages reveal that ELL students schooled in one-way and two-way dual language programs meet or exceed the grade-level scores in English by Grade 5, and grade-level achievement is sustained through high school graduation. The same level is also achieved in students' first language. Reportedly, students from these DL programs represent fewer dropouts than those students in traditional programs (Collier & Thomas, 2009).

The decision to implement a DL program is a long-term programming and financial commitment. Districts must be able to hire capable and qualified teachers proficient in the ELLs' first language. There must be a pool of teachers to cover all grade levels. Comparable and ancillary materials are needed in both languages of instruction. At the building level, common planning time for teams of DL teachers is essential. The DL programming is a commitment to continued quality education of all students.

Sheltered Instruction/the Sheltered Instruction Observation Protocol (SIOP) Model

For some school districts a DL program is not feasible. They may have a very language-diverse population with no one language in the majority. Or they may have ELLs who represent only one language, for example Urdu, but there is a lack of qualified bilingual Urdu teachers. Additionally, state teacher education certification programs may not grant certifications in the first language of the ELL population. In these cases a reasonable and more flexible option is the use of Sheltered Instruction, an approach to providing access to mainstream, grade-level content while promoting the development of English-language proficiency. Another option is Sheltered Instruction Observation Protocol (SIOP), a research-based model of lesson planning for delivering Sheltered Instruction. An outgrowth of content-based ESL instruction, SIOP's goal is "to teach content to students learning English through a developmental language approach" (Echevarría, Vogt, & Short, 2008, p.13). In this model, ELLs are given more time and support to learn English, and at the same time they learn the content necessary to progress through the grades and graduate. A unique characteristic of the SIOP model is that ELLs are taught the content in English by content-area teachers, not ESL specialists. SIOP instruction creates a bridge linking English-language acquisition with content learning (Echevarría et al., 2008).

Versatility is also a characteristic of a SIOP-driven program. Sheltered Instruction (SI) can easily be incorporated into the existing structure and curriculum of a school. The SI approach can be incorporated in two-way dual language programs, late exit transition programs, ESL programs, newcomer programs, and even foreign-language immersion programs. The class composition can be all ELLs or a mixture of native speakers and nonnative speakers of English. The SIOP protocol is made up of thirty different features that fit into eight main components that enhance and extend teachers' pedagogy to teach content to ELLs. The eight components are lesson preparation, building background, comprehensible input, strategies, interaction, practice or application, lesson delivery, and review or assessment (Echevarría et al., 2008). Content teachers can use their content-knowledge expertise in the SIOP framework of how to teach it to ELLs (Echevarría et al., 2008).

Response to Intervention (RTI)

Along with the requirements and regulations of No Child Left Behind and Common Core State Standards, schools must demonstrate the progress of all students through the tiered intervention model of Response to Intervention (RTI). The goal of the RTI model is to identify students at risk early and provide the appropriate interventions. Usually a three-tiered model of progressively more intense academic support for those identified students, the unique feature of RTI is that the first level of intervention is in the classroom with the classroom teacher. This requires the teacher to document, monitor, and assess at-risk students' progress using research-based strategies. Academic success is intrinsically tied to language in American schools. Learning is measured by way of listening, speaking, reading, and writing English. English language learners often exhibit the same difficulties with learning as children with learning disabilities do. Therefore, it is important to identify ELL students who are at risk as soon as possible and discern whether the problem is one of second-language acquisition or one related to a disability.

While the basic structure of tiered intervention applies to the identification of ELLs, school districts often find the challenge of how to best serve culturally and linguistically diverse students an overwhelming charge. At each level, both the assessment and the instruction or intervention should be culturally and linguistically appropriate (Brown & Doolittle, 2008).

RTI Tier 1: Universal screening. During this tier of RTI, the classroom teacher assesses individual student growth over time to determine whether students are progressing as expected. Paramount in this tier is the classroom teacher's appreciation of ELLs' culture and language. These are assets to value and build on during instruction. When screening ELLs at this level, there should be a match between the child's needs and the instructional program. The ELLs' progress should be compared to their peers. For ELLs, their real peers may not be the other children in their class. ELLs should be compared to those students who have similar cultural, linguistic, and educational backgrounds. Language skills in both native and second languages need to be assessed (Brown & Doolittle, 2008; National Center on Response to Intervention, 2011). Additionally, to successfully identify and instruct ELL students at risk, classroom teachers need some basic knowledge of second-language acquisition. Here are some basic key factors:

- Language learning is a developmental process, and errors are a natural part of development.
- Well-developed literacy in one's first language facilitates the transfer of skills and language development to one's second language.
- ELLs may be proficient in basic interpersonal communication skills (BICS) but lack cognitive academic linguistic proficiency (CALP).
- It takes five to seven years to acquire a second language to the proficiency level equal to that of same-aged peers (Collier, 1987; Cummins, 1984).

Figure 5.1 outlines some guidelines suggested by Salend and Salinas (2003) for distinguishing between a language difference and a language disability.

Once a scientifically based intervention has been identified, the foundation of the instruction should be culturally responsive. Some characteristics of culturally responsive instruction are building on ELLs' background knowledge, providing linguistic instruction on language forms and functions, implementing strategies that use visuals, modeling, and providing native-language instruction (Brown & Doolittle, 2008).

Figure 5.1   Response to Intervention (RTI) Guidelines for Identifying
English Language Learner (ELL) Students at Risk

Recommendation	Rationale
Diversify the evaluation team	Looks at child from many points of view
Offer training to evaluation team	Widens options for interventions
Compare student performance in both native language and English	Helps distinguish learning or language issues
Consider components of second-language acquisition	Helps distinguish learning or language issues
Include nontraditional testing	Provides more complete profile of student
Include student's life experiences that affect learning	Illuminates cultural and experiential factors
Use data analysis to develop intervention	Drives relevant and effective instruction

Source: Adapted from Salend & Salinas, 2003, p. 36.

RTI Tier 2: More intensive instruction. If learners do not meet the
anticipated progress in Tier 1, they move to Tier 2, where they
receive small-group intensive instruction by a specialist. Tier 2
instruction is in addition to the general education instruction the
student receives, not instead of the general instruction. The more
intensive instruction of Tier 2 still needs to be culturally and linguistically responsive and should assess ELLs' progress in relation to
other ELLs' real peers. Instruction often focuses on reading. The
development of vocabulary and oracy skills, along with reading
skills, is recommended for this tier (Vaughn & Ortiz, n.d.). The
ELL's progress should be observed in multiple settings and with
varied activities (Brown & Doolittle, 2008).

RTI Tier 3: Intensive individualized instruction. If learners do not
meet the anticipated progress of Tier 1 and Tier 2, they move to Tier
3, where they receive intense, explicit, and individualized instruction. A specialist, such as a bilingual educator, special educator, or
ESL teacher, provides this instruction (Vaughn & Ortiz, n.d.). The
instruction should continue to be culturally and linguistically
appropriate. If the school is beginning the process of providing special education services, parent permission might be required. The
concept of special education might be unfamiliar or taboo to the
parents of ELLs. Therefore, the implementation of a team approach
to problem solving is advantageous.

While implementing RTI with ELLs can be a challenge, it can also be an opportunity for schoolwide collaboration and in-house professional development. As the nation shifts to the Common Core State Standards, the strategies and best practices used to instruct ELLs require teachers to expand their repertoire of needed skills. Yet the teaching strategies used for ELLs are applicable for all students, regardless of race or ethnicity.

Before- and After-School Programs

On a smaller scale, instead of implementing a DL program, applying the SI approach, or augmenting the RTI model, schools and their districts can offer additional support to ELLs in before- and after-school programs. Such programs can provide a range of enrichment or intervention to ELLs, either long- or short-term, and usually for a specific area. Some examples of before- and after-school programs help with content-area development, language development through the arts, and homework. Once again, the programs should address the needs of the school district and its schools.

Content area development. Content area before- and after-school programs usually target a specific content area need of the student, such as literacy or math. They can be utilized as a form of intervention or enrichment.

At Park Avenue School in Port Chester, New York, a student teacher from Manhattanville College team taught with her special education cooperating teachers a before-school math program for ELLs and students identified as at risk. She provided small-group instruction on computation skills and the vocabulary of math. This before-school program provided targeted instruction and a social context for ELLs to use verbal and written English skills to learn mathematical concepts.

An after-school science program, Healthy Neighborhoods/ Healthy Kids (Tillman, 2007) at R. J. Bailey School in Greenburgh 7, New York, a CSI school, offered a refreshing perspective to the traditional after-school remediation model. HNHK was offered as an enrichment program. Manhattanville professor Sherie McClam explored the school neighborhood with a group of fourth, fifth, and sixth graders interested in science and the environment using place-based and problem-based learning. Placed-based learning requires students to reflect on and define their space in the school setting. The students created a needs-assessment instrument of the school cafeteria. The assessment required students to collaborate as a group and express a point of view. Beyond the opportunity for expressive language development, the project prompted discussion about acculturation issues and cultural clashes. One Pakistani student remarked that an improvement to the school cafeteria would be to play soft music and paint the walls. It appeared that in her mind this American school cafeteria was not conducive to healthful eating because it did not provide the familiar environment of going home at lunchtime to share the meal in the company of family. This project improved school community and promoted students' excitement about problem solving.

Arts-based programs. Arts-based programs are usually considered enrichment programs, but for ELLs, they are perhaps essential. An arts-based program affords an opportunity to express ideas and knowledge in a different way from traditional school assignments. First Lady Michelle Obama stated in her address at the opening spring gala of the American Ballet, "Learning through the arts reinforces critical academic skills in reading, language arts, and math and provides students with the skills to creatively solve problems" (Obama, 2009, para. 1).

The after-school drama club at George Washington School in White Plains, New York, brought native-English speakers and ELL students together. Not only did the program give additional academic support to the ELLs through listening, speaking, and reading English for an audience, but it also socially integrated two segments of the school population, ELLs and mainstream general education students.

Homework helper. Homework-helper programs offer small-group and individual help in academics to ELLs. A bonus element of these school programs is that one-on-one and small groups allow the ELL students to find a voice in a social context and address their individual questions and misconceptions.

Summer Programs

One advantage of summer programs is that they reduce the academic loss of knowledge that occurs during the students' prolonged time out of the school environment. Research shows that students' achievement test scores drop between the spring assessment and the first assessment the following fall (Allington, 2006). Summer programs provide continuity throughout the entire year.

A twist to summer programs began at George Washington School in White Plains, New York, when ESL teachers observed a new phenomenon in their changing suburban school population. When they reviewed the data from the annual screening of incoming kindergarteners, they noticed that a significant number of incoming Spanish-speaking kindergarteners scored well below expectations. These children were already experiencing the achievement gap before they entered school. With ingenuity and limited resources, the teachers applied for and received a grant to provide workshops in Spanish for Hispanic parents on preliteracy readiness skills. The Kindergarten-Providing Academic Skills and Strategy program (K-PASS) gave Hispanic parents the tools to be literacy partners, filling the void for their children who were not able to attend a preschool program. The success of the program prompted the district to expand the program to its other elementary schools (Gómez, Lang, & Lasser, 2010). Another CSI district learned about the K-PASS program through the CSI Consortium and has adapted it to fit its unique needs for children entering the DL program in the fall.

The CSI school districts are innovators and problem solvers. At all levels, elementary, middle, and high school, the districts have gathered data, analyzed the data, and established programs to meet the challenges of educating a changing population. Figure 5.2 provides examples of some of their successful programs and the reasons for their success.

Assessment of Programs

Presumably, much thought and research occur before a program is initiated in a school or district. In a general sense, any program is implemented with the overarching purpose of improving the effectiveness of a school or district. The specific programs employed are based on the unique characteristics of change of the specific school or district. Once implemented, the program needs to be assessed to see if the goals and purposes are being achieved. Much like Lewin's (1946) cyclic review of the action research used by classroom teachers, programs can be assessed in the same manner. The four basic steps to solving a problem are to plan, act, observe, and reflect (Kendell, 2009). Assessing programs in this manner allows for input from all stakeholders in developing a successful program.

Establishing Purpose for Assessment

Assessing for the sake of assessing wastes precious schooltime and resources. The first step in assessing a program is to have a purpose for the assessment. Why do you want to assess the program?

Figure 5.2   Examples of Programs Implemented for ELLs by School
Leaders and Reasons for Their Success

School Level	Program Implemented	Reasons for Success
Elementary	• Newcomer Center • Dual language (Spanish) • Dual language (Italian) • Summer enrichment • Sheltered Instruction Observation Protocol (SIOP) • Full-service community school	• Quick acculturation to U.S. schools • Parental buy-in for bilingualism • Promotes heritage language of the community and parental buy-in • Closes the achievement gap • English instruction for heterogeneous English as a second language classes, does not require bilingual teachers • Educates whole child and families and creates parent participation at school
Middle schools	• Newcomer Center • After-school content program	• Quick acculturation to U.S. schools • Provides enrichment and academic support
High schools	• Students with interrupted formal education (SIFE) • After-school content program	• Provides intensive literacy instruction • Provides enrichment and academic support

Often the answer is to see if it is successful. The next question then is how we measure success. Establishing criteria yields useful data. Once the criteria are set, the instruments for measurement can be decided.

When assessing programs related to ELLs, the specific curriculum needs must be considered along with knowledge of second-language acquisition. Many districts assess reading comprehension by using assessment instruments from commercial reading programs to determine reading levels. Most standardized-testing instruments were designed and normed on middle-class native speakers of English. Both types of assessments put ELLs at a disadvantage, and the data can be easily overgeneralized (Echevarría & Vogt, 2011). We need to go back to the questions about why we want to assess the program and how we can best measure success. Sometimes the assessments can be given in the child's native language. Other times, formative assessments reveal more valuable information about the success of a program.

Gathering Data

To evaluate a program, data are necessary from all stakeholders of the program. At the school level, program assessment data should be gathered from administrators, teachers, support staff, parents, and the students involved in the program. Each constituency offers a different and valid perspective of the program. An additional data point to be considered is the cost-effectiveness of the program. Administrators generally need to justify the cost of a particular program. Rich data support the cause.

Using Findings to Strengthen Program Development

Just as schools and districts use data to drive instruction, so should data support the development and assessment of programs. Let the data set speak for itself. Going back to the cyclic action research model, it is important to reflect and plan the next programming steps.

Guidelines for School Leaders

The changing demographics and the demands of legislative regulations and requirements present many challenges for schools and school districts. Dealing with ELLs can be new, but it is not an insurmountable challenge. Some guidelines to providing programs and services for ELLs and their families are presented below.

Determine Instruction in Relation to Student Needs

Before any program or service can be implemented, articulate the problem or need. Begin with a needs assessment for your unique environment. Be sure to include input from all parties: administrators, teachers, support staff, parents, and students. Some questions to consider are as follows: What is the problem? How do I measure it?

Guidelines for School Leaders

- Determine instruction in relation to student needs
- Delineate roles and responsibilities of school leaders and teachers
- Promote positive interaction in the school and community

Is there already a program to address our needs? Who would implement it? How do I get all stakeholders involved? What resources are necessary? What is the cost?

Consider ways to encourage parents of ELLs to participate. This may mean that information must be transmitted bilingually or in face-to-face meetings with a facilitator who speaks the same language as the parent. Research the educational goal. Investigate existing commercial programs for ELLs. Connect with neighboring districts with similar demographics. What are they doing? What has worked for them? Assess personnel and financial resources. Determine whether bilingual teachers are needed. Collect all possible data, and devise an informed plan for a program.

Delineate Roles and Responsibilities of School Leaders and Teachers

The major role of school leaders and teachers is to collaborate in creating an educational environment that embraces and values diversity. Fundamental to this responsibility is to eliminate the view that ELLs need to be fixed or remediated (Collier & Thomas, 2009). They need to be educated.

Discuss ideas about cultural diversity with the staff. Though this might be difficult and uncomfortable, clearing the air lets you evaluate what types of professional development programs are necessary for the successful teaching and learning of ELLs. If the faculty and administrators are basically English speaking and white, a starting point could be to read and discuss as a group Peg McIntosh's (1988) *White Privilege: Unpacking the Invisible Knapsack* (available online at http://nymbp.org/reference/WhitePrivilege.pdf).

Develop a school language policy. Cummins (2001) listed some questions to ask about school language. Some examples are as follows:

> Does the school's language policy articulate the benefit of all recognizing and exploring language diversity? Does it make a strong commitment to home-language development? . . . Are all school staff (including assessment specialists and special education personnel) made aware of the school's language policy and invited to discuss its provisions and make contribution to its improvement? (p. 316)

Become knowledgeable about second-language acquisition. Fundamental are the concepts of basic interpersonal communication skills (BICS) and cognitive academic linguistic proficiency (CALP) and the length of time it takes to become proficient in a second language (mentioned above in this chapter).

Incorporate curricula that acknowledge and value the home languages of ELLs. This can be accomplished in small and big ways. At the classroom level, word walls can include the home languages of the students (if it is a written language). The classroom library collection should offer both window and mirror books representing the cultures and languages of the students. On a schoolwide level, offer bilingual and DL programs. Make morning announcements bilingual, trilingual, or beyond to include the home languages of the ELLs.

Incorporate and develop curricula that purposefully develop both English-language skills and content-area concepts and material. SIOP is one way to do this. A strong understanding of second-language acquisition processes and theories is fundamental for both teachers and school leaders. This knowledge gives teachers the background necessary to construct instruction that matches the students' levels of English proficiency while continuing to move forward with content-area curricula. These curricula should also be culturally appropriate and relevant to the students, the parents, and their backgrounds. Tapping into the students' background, culture, and knowledge base, though different from English-dominant students, facilitates forward movement through curricula.

Promote Positive Interaction in the School and Community

Just as buy-in from the teachers for servicing an ELL population is important, so is buy-in from parents and the school community. At the outset, the voices of the community must be recognized and heard. All groups of stakeholders should participate in aspects of the process when planning changes in the school's programs and instruction for ELLs. The first step is to inform and educate the community about the reasons and justifications for the programs or changes. The members of the school community potentially offer different points of view about the issues. Logically, as stakeholders in what happens at school, members of the school community can facilitate or inhibit desired changes planned for the education of ELLs. To bring the community on board with desired changes, they must feel as though their opinions and concerns matter. A collaborative decision-making process empowers parents of ELLs. The sense of empowerment of the parents can transfer to the children and result in positive academic achievements (Cummins, 2001).

As mentioned previously in this chapter, the development of a DL program began from a request by parents of the school community.

Now in its third year, the DL program has a waiting list. The consequences of not participating in shared decision making with the school community can lead to confrontational responses from the school community. Finnish parents in Sweden organized a strike when the headmistress unilaterally reduced the hours of instruction of Finnish (Cummins, 2001). When the education of ELLs is viewed as a positive experience and decision making involves all stakeholders, it is a win-win situation for all parties: administrators, teachers, parents, students, and the community at large.

Concluding Remarks

The days of monolingualism and homogeneity in school districts have given way to a tapestry of cultural and linguistic diversity. School districts that embrace diversity, develop programs that are based on the principles of second-language acquisition, and celebrate the cultural background of their ELL population usually promote academic success for ELLs. School leaders need to reflect on their own views and values related to culture and language as well as those of their teachers and parents. Academic gains for ELLs are achieved through many venues: programs, culturally responsive instruction, teacher preparation, professional development, and collaborative decision making. Creating a new tapestry to include the many valuable assets of an ELL population provides success for all students and the whole-school community.

6

School–University Collaboration

For years, a local elementary school principal tried to get her very talented and dedicated first- and second-grade teachers to use technology with their children. In addition to believing in technology as an important tool for developing the children's skills, the principal knew that her superintendent was a technology enthusiast who was paying increasingly more attention to those schools that were supporting his focus for the district. This principal had been successful in persuading her upper-elementary teachers to use technology, but she could not budge her primary teachers.

At the same time, the director of a center for education at a local university was feeling pressure to do something more substantial to ensure that teacher candidates left the program with the ability to integrate technology into teaching. This director and principal recently had signed a formal agreement to have the principal's school serve as a professional development school (PDS). One of the first things that the principal told the director was that, while her school and the district had a reputation for being technologically savvy, she needed to do something about her primary teachers.

Together, they decided that they would create a plan that would require teacher candidates, university supervisors, and primary teachers to work together to teach technology-based lessons. Coincidentally, their state had just issued a request for proposal (RFP) for schools and colleges to work together to develop, implement, and assess technology *initiatives to improve K–12 students' learning. The principal, director, and other team members quickly wrote a proposal that required their primary teachers and teacher candidates to coteach eight technology-based lessons within a student-teaching semester. University supervisors would be required to work closely with the teacher candidates and cooperating teachers to assist and ensure that the lessons were taught. The grant application was funded for $250,000, enabling the director and principal to provide portable computer labs for their primary teachers, portable computers for their teacher candidates, instructional materials, and a series of workshops to prepare the teachers, teacher candidates, and university supervisors to use the technology. Within a year, the primary teachers were using computers on their own, the teacher candidates understood how and when to use technology to enrich students' learning, and the primary children were showing positive changes in their literacy development because of the multiple ways in which they were practicing skill development. The principal and director attributed their success to their partnership because they listened to each other, planned accordingly, and went after the necessary resources to implement their plan. Neither could have done it without the other, and they knew it (Wepner, Bowes, & Serotkin, 2007).*

Administrators often loathe the idea of yet another project or responsibility that costs additional time and money without obvious benefits. Although school–university partnerships cannot guarantee short-term results, they can bring about immediate changes and evolve into long-term and sustainable positive outcomes for both schools and schools of education.

Reasons for School–University Collaborations

School–university partnerships embody the essence of collaboration and have been cited as the most frequently recommended approach to educational reform (Dyson, 1999; Olson, 1987). The idea of school–university collaborations has existed for the past 100 years (Greene & Tichenor, 1999), but many have faded into oblivion because the unique needs of each institution were not addressed (Peel, Peel, & Baker, 2002). Many also have focused on urban schools for improved student achievement (e.g., Rothstein, 2001; Walker, Downey, & Cox-Henderson, 2010).

Attention now needs to be given to forming school–university partnerships to address the changing student population of suburban school districts. Teacher education programs are beginning to show how they are using field experiences and methods courses to help teacher candidates become aware of culturally responsive teaching in suburban school districts (Downey & Cobbs, 2007). Educational leaders in suburban school districts are discovering for themselves the short-term and long-term rewards of working closely with their higher-education neighbors.

This chapter provides an overview of the benefits and challenges of school–university partnerships, describes partnership examples from Changing Suburbs Institute (CSI) districts and other suburban school districts, and offers guidelines for developing such partnerships.

There are three main reasons to pursue school–university partnerships: professional development, student achievement, and administrative staffing needs.

Professional Development

Our profession is a profession because, as educators responsible for students' learning, we never stop learning about new and improved curriculum ideas and instructional methods that can positively affect students' achievement. Educational leaders, as pivotal persons for their schools' success, are responsible for ensuring that their teaching staff have access to and participate in professional development opportunities. School–university partnerships are a useful resource for professional development. Especially useful is the creation of a professional development school (PDS), as noted in the opening vignette. A PDS is a school that partners with a college or university to provide professional development for teachers, prepare teacher candidates, improve student achievement, and encourage practitioner inquiry. PDS partners share responsibilities for professional development and blend their expertise and resources to meet shared goals.

The PDSs can have the following benefits: raise the level of teacher expectation and student work; increase the student–teacher ratio; expose teachers to new and enhanced methodology; increase teacher leadership; offer innovative and cutting-edge ideas that teachers can use and apply; stimulate collaborative inquiry about practice; cultivate students' improved attitude toward learning; offer new and exciting dialogues about teaching and learning; infuse new blood into the building; and help with teacher renewal.

PDSs are not for teachers' professional development only. Principals' roles and responsibilities are actually redefined as they develop and experiment with a new organizational culture that supports collaborative work with university partners (Stroble & Luka, 1999). Principals also need to be able to take advantage of professional development opportunities. When K–12 teachers and administrators and university faculty and administrators can sit side by side in professional development opportunities, such as those described below, they begin to think and work together on ways to build their collaborative initiatives.

On-site coursework by university faculty. University faculty are willing to come to a school or district to offer courses.

Assistant Superintendent Lenora Boehlert (see her thoughts in Box 6.1) and Shelley Wepner, Dean and Professor of Education at Manhattanville College, agreed on a specific tuition discount for on-site coursework in TESOL because of their pre-existing partnership agreement and worked with the college's graduate advisement office to schedule the appropriate courses on a convenient day and time at the local school. Teachers who successfully completed the sequence of courses became eligible for an additional certification.

Coteaching with university faculty at a school site also becomes possible. Shelley had the pleasure a while back of coteaching a writing course with a seventh-grade language arts teacher at a changing suburban junior high school. The seventh-, eighth-, and ninth-grade language arts teachers knew that they needed to be refreshed and updated on ways to teach and promote writing, especially for students with learning challenges, yet did not want to travel to the university to take a course. The junior high school's English department chair worked with the college to make the arrangements to offer the

---

Box 6.1   From the Assistant Superintendent's Desk on Onsite Coursework

Lenora Boehlert, Assistant Superintendent of White Plains School District in New York, approached Manhattanville College to schedule a series of graduate courses for the district's teachers, specifically in teaching English as a second language (TESOL). Lenora works in a large, diverse suburban school district, and she no longer wants her teachers to submit for reimbursement courses offered by for-profit companies that have very little to do with their primary areas of responsibility. She wants her teachers to engage in substantive coursework that can be applied to what they are actually doing.

course at the school. Because the coteacher knew the teachers, who knew each other, and knew the junior high school students, the assignments for this credit-bearing graduate course were adapted to meet teachers' needs.

On-site coursework by K–12 teachers and administrators. With the incentive of not having to travel, K–12 teachers and administrators can work with colleges and universities to arrange to teach credit-bearing courses. A principal of one of CSI's professional development schools knew that her teachers needed to better understand how to work with parents of the school's special needs students. Because of her own background in special education, she worked with the chair of the college's special education department to arrange to become an adjunct faculty member for the purpose of teaching the course at her school to her own teachers and interested teachers across the district.

Coteaching with university faculty. From elementary school through high school, coteaching with university faculty has become an important source of professional development for both classroom teachers and university faculty because of the give-and-take exchange of both theoretical and practical ideas. A social studies teacher educator, intent on having his students spend most of their time in the schools for his course, reached out to a middle school social studies teacher to invite himself and his students to the social studies classroom. In exchange for this privilege, he agreed to coteach a few lessons to demonstrate how to use his newly published theory of instruction to motivate middle school students to learn. In return, the social studies teacher helped this social studies teacher educator and his students to learn firsthand about the many challenges of working with diverse student needs.

A teacher educator responsible for teaching elementary science methods wanted her teacher candidates to spend most of the semester in an elementary classroom to help them discover that the teaching of science does not have to be feared or ignored. She approached a second-grade teacher from one of CSI's professional development schools that agreed to host the teacher candidates. The faculty member worked with her teacher candidates and the second-grade teacher to plan units of instruction, purchase science materials, and develop a schedule that allowed for classroom teacher and college faculty, classroom teacher and teacher candidate, and college faculty and teacher candidate instruction. When the teacher candidates were not teaching, they were observing and/or working in small student groups to ensure that the second-grade students had hands-on experience. The second-grade students had every possible opportunity to experiment with the science concepts as the adults in the room took turns providing direct instruction. The second-grade teacher has since become a spokesperson for this method of instruction and wants to help other classroom teachers branch out to work with university faculty and students.

Action research. A principal discovered that her second-grade students do not bully each other in the playground, even though she thought that this was a problem in her school. A high school principal learned how to promote integrity in his high school. Another high school principal learned how to reduce high school tardiness with time-management training. An elementary teacher learned about the effects of playing slow-tempo music during poetry writing. As discussed in Chapter 4, action research, whether conducted by classroom teachers, teacher candidates, or college faculty, is a powerful mechanism for testing hypotheses about learning and leading in classrooms and schools. Action research does take time and expertise. University partners can provide college faculty to assist classroom teachers so that they can conduct their own research and/or provide teacher candidates to conduct or co-conduct action research with classroom teachers. For instance, a faculty member worked with four middle school teacher volunteers at one of CSI's professional development schools on action-research projects that they designed to answer questions about their own classroom practices in science, foreign language, and physical education. Action research can also be conducted by principals to determine their own leadership practices. Principals who engage in their own action research about themselves engage in meaningful professional development that impacts their own practices (Dana, Tricarico, & Quinn, 2010).

Faculty research with K–12 teachers. Four teachers in an elementary school were highlighted in an article in a peer-reviewed journal because of their role in conducting research on the shifting roles and responsibilities of teachers when implementing technology in the classroom (Wepner & Tao, 2002). A primary school administrator coauthored an article and a chapter with two faculty members on the influence of parent education on kindergarten children's achievement (Gómez, Lang, & Lasser, 2010; Lang, Gómez, Lasser, 2009). An elementary principal coauthored an article about a special project to implement a science-based literacy project with fifth-grade students (Wepner, Bettica, Gangi, Reilly, Klemm, 2008). Conducting research, often reserved for those in higher education because of job expectations, is a form of professional development that expands one's understandings of how to test new ideas and answer questions about instructional and leadership practices.

Grants. The vignette at the beginning of this chapter describes how a principal worked with her local university to get a grant for her school that provided equipment and professional development for her teachers. She believes that this grant transformed her primary teachers, with one in particular who hated technology and then became an avid user. School–university partnerships make it easier for both institutions to apply for grants, especially today, because of the national recognition from legislators, policymakers, politicians, and corporate leaders that K–12 and higher education must be interconnected to make inroads on student achievement.

K–12 teachers and administrators teach at the university. After buying into the concept of being part of one of CSI's professional development schools, two fifth-grade teachers determined that this new school designation enabled them to teach a graduate course in children's literature. They had years of experience identifying and using books that appealed to their multicultural student population. They worked with their partner college's literacy department to become hired as adjunct faculty and worked with the chair of the department to make sure that they understood how to combine theory with practice and how to appeal to the wider graduate student population. These two teachers found that this teaching experience was an intense and rewarding form of professional development.

An elementary school principal of a professional development school realized that the PDS required her to begin thinking again about reasons she had chosen this field and reasons for her decisions to help her students achieve. For years, she had been consumed with day-to-day administrative responsibilities of the job and had not allowed herself the luxury of thinking about the reasons behind leadership decision making. The partnership required her to participate in meetings and events at the college with other principals, faculty, and teachers. Within a year of becoming a PDS principal, she discovered that she had much to offer graduate students in the educational leadership program and was hired as an adjunct faculty member to teach a course and serve as a clinical supervisor of practicum. Students in the program loved her because, as a practicing administrator, she could help them balance theory with practice. She loved her new role because, as she delved into the literature and interacted with graduate students, she was learning how to better balance practice with theory.

Presentations at a university. Showcasing the work from a school–university partnership brings key players together to plan and present, reinforces the efforts of those involved, and communicates to others in the community just how fruitful the partnership is. Some examples include a panel of principals speaking about the promises and challenges of forming PDSs; an elementary principal speaking about how a partnership can transform a school; a middle school principal speaking about the value of doing fieldwork at the middle school level; a high school teacher speaking about the benefits of an after-school math club begun by a university professor and his students; a panel of assistant superintendents speaking about ways in which university interns have found jobs in their districts; a group of K–12 teachers speaking about their experience working with university faculty and its impact on their students; and faculty and teachers speaking about their experiences with implementing projects in social studies, science, and math. Such presentations reflect well on the school district and promote yet another level of professional development.

Presentations at conferences with university faculty. The informal and formal research conducted by teachers and administrators through school–university partnerships provides opportunities to attend and present at conferences. Since all of this book's authors have been involved with partnerships, we personally have presented with dozens of K–12 faculty and administrators at local, regional, and national conferences. Conference attendance, usually supported by school districts and universities, enables representatives from both types of institutions to have critical dialogues about ways to improve instruction.

The professional development opportunities described above contribute to teachers' and principals' development. Research on teacher development (Bullough & Baughman, 1997) in school–university partnerships, especially PDSs, indicate that teachers have a sense of renewal and rejuvenation by learning from teacher education candidates and university supervisors over an extended period of time. They become more reflective about teaching and, as a result, change their classroom practice. Teachers become part of a learning community that dialogues, asks questions, works together to achieve something for themselves and their students, and probes about their own practices.

The survey in Figure 6.1 can help superintendents and principals know the level at which their teachers are engaged with a university to help with their own professional development. The survey can be useful before a partnership with a university is even formed. Some teachers might be teaching as adjuncts and using the university's library and fitness facilities, others might be serving as cooperating teachers and hosting university students for fieldwork, and others might be working with university faculty to get help with their classroom. Results from the survey reveal individual and collective levels of involvement and help determine which teachers can help other teachers get involved and the type of involvement that should be encouraged. For example, before one CSI school became a PDS, one of the teachers from that school had already been involved with Manhattanville College on eight different survey items and ended up serving as a spokesperson for the partnership.

Student Achievement

Research on the impact of school–university partnerships on student achievement continues to grow. The achievement of K–12 students on a state mandated achievement test increased after their schools became a part of the Houston Consortium (Houston, Hollis, Clay, Ligons, & Roff, 1999). A longitudinal study that investigated the impact of a PDS on teaching practices and student learning over a five-year period indicated that as teaching practices improved, student learning improved (Castle, Rockwood, & Tortora, 2008).

A study of a partnership with a university, a community college, and a public school district indicated that K–12 student achievement in mathematics and reading improved in three out of four PDS schools (Walker, Sorensen, Smaldino, & Downey, 2008). Student achievement was cited most frequently as a perceived advantage of school–university partnerships in a study of a partnership between one Chicago university and ten Chicago public schools (Borthwick, Stirling, Nauman, & Cook, 2003).

When university faculty and students are given the opportunity to work directly with both teachers and K–12 students, exciting possibilities arise as a result of new curriculum ideas, instructional methodologies, materials, and management tools. The additional persons attending to the needs of classroom teachers and their students also contribute significantly to changes in performance and attitude. Superintendents and principals clearly benefit by reaching out to universities to take advantage of the resources available to them. Options are described below that highlight ways that university faculty and students can help promote student achievement.

Figure 6.1   Survey for K–12 Educators

Survey for K–12 Educators	Yes	No	Not Sure
Serve as a cooperating teacher			
Work with university students for fieldwork			
Work with university students for literacy practicum			
Work with university faculty and students on field-based courses			
Use university students for tutoring students			
Use university students as pen pals or electronic pals			
Use university students for small-group work			
Coteach with university faculty in K–12 or university classroom			
Teach at a university			
Attend university events (conferences, workshops, symposia, lectures, etc.)			
Work on a committee or advisory board at a university			
Work with university faculty and/or administration on special projects (if yes, please describe)			
Work with university faculty or administration on research (if yes, please describe)			
Involved in a partnership or professional development school with a university			
Use university resources (library, fitness facilities, conference rooms, etc.)			
Serve on leadership team in your school and/or school district that involves university faculty			
Bring or send students to a university for visitations and/or university forums			
Attend professional development sessions with university faculty to help with instruction, content knowledge, or other areas of interest			
Communicate with university faculty through e-mail about something related to your job			
Work with university faculty and/or administration to get help with your classroom, school, or district			

University faculty work directly with students at school or at university. University faculty want and need to work with K–12 students to help in general and stay current for their own students and themselves.

A favorite example involves three college faculty members, two from education and one from biology, who put together a creative science, literacy, and arts project for 100 fifth-grade students at their school (mentioned earlier in this chapter). This cross-curricular learning experience involved literacy development through storytelling, science learning through forensic exploration, and learning of the arts through finger painting and poetry. The faculty went separate times to the school to work with the students during a four-month period. A survey administered to the students indicated that the project increased their engagement with learning science and using storytelling and the arts to help them further develop their literacy skills. The fifth-grade teachers expressed satisfaction with their students' experiences. This project arose as a result of the principal's outreach and involvement with the college and subsequent funding by a foundation interested in working with a school–university partnership (Wepner et al., 2008).

University faculty also are very willing to work with students at the university, especially when it involves their own areas of expertise. The principal mentioned in the opening vignette wanted to expose her students to the university setting so that her students would see college as part of their future. This principal worked with the education director, who in turn worked with education and liberal arts faculty to put together a science day for fifth graders, a social studies day for fourth graders, and an arts day for third graders. The school district funded busing to transport students to the university on their designated day. The university provided the faculty, the materials for instruction, and a special lunch in the university cafeteria (the highlight of the day!). Science Day had faculty from education, biology, chemistry, and physics providing workshops for the students. Social Studies Day had faculty from education, history, and political science providing workshops on elections and citizenship. Arts Day had faculty from education, the art department, the theater department, and the music department providing workshops on photography, theater, music, and drawing. These special days prompted classroom teachers, elementary students, teacher candidates, liberal arts faculty, education faculty, parents, school district administrators, and university administrators to work together to develop unique learning opportunities for many potential first-generation college attendees.

University students work directly with students. One of the best-kept secrets is the availability of assistance, often free, from university students who need and want to be involved in schools for fieldwork and community-outreach activities. Teacher candidates need to clock hours to fulfill course and program requirements. Other university students are required and/or encouraged to engage in service learning and other community-service initiatives.

University students can help with tutoring students before, during, and after school. An elementary principal worked with her college liaison to arrange for tutoring across her school for different subject areas. A high school department chair of mathematics worked with his college liaison to arrange an after-school mathematics tutoring program for students having trouble in the classroom. University students can help with homework in before- and after-school programs. A middle school principal worked with a college to arrange an after-school "homework helper" program for students in the sixth, seventh, and eighth grades. With a little funding, special programs can be developed. Some schools work with their university partners to arrange intern programs for teacher candidates who serve as substitute teachers. Interns can be hired for a half year or an entire year to serve as substitutes when needed and spend the remainder of their time assisting teachers with one-on-one, small-group, and whole-class instruction. Sometimes these interns spend the equivalent of one university semester as student teachers and the remainder of the time as substitute teachers. Different configurations can be created to fit the needs of the schools. For example, interns can be hired to provide time for teachers to have one day a week away from teaching duties to assume an alternative role such as researcher, student teacher supervisor, or administrative intern (Boles, 1992).

Other programs can also be created. An elementary principal hired a university student from the theater department to begin a drama club for her fourth- and fifth-grade students. A middle school principal hired a few students from the dance department to create an after-school dance program. So much depends on the connections made between the school and the university and the ability of both a K–12 school leader and a university liaison to identify the types of programs that are needed. From straight academics to the arts, the involvement of university students with K–12 students contributes to students' learning and positively affects their attitude toward learning.

University faculty and university students work directly with students. As stated earlier, teacher education faculty need to be in the schools for their own credibility. Liberal arts and science faculty want to be in the schools because of their own sense of social justice. When university faculty bring their students to the schools to work directly with K–12 students, there is newfound excitement and energy that translate into student achievement differences.

A classic example for teacher education programs is the use of field-based methodology courses, where teacher education faculty arrange with one or more teachers to have their students come to their classrooms to learn how to teach in specific content areas or for specific purposes. While many models exist, the most noteworthy courses require coteaching by the university faculty member, classroom teacher, and teacher education candidates. Coteaching requires in-depth awareness of the content and concepts to be taught as well as instructional and assessment know-how of the coteachers. As different adult pairs coteach, others in the classroom assist the students with their work. Although field-based courses require that classroom teachers adjust their teaching methods, they soon learn different ideas and methodologies that strengthen their teaching. Field-based methods courses are very useful for preparing teacher candidates to teach with diverse students, especially in changing suburban schools where there are many students whose first language is not English. As one teacher candidate expressed in her self-evaluation, "It really helped me to learn how to teach diverse children and better understand how to work with language differences."

During-school, after-school, and summer programs also lend themselves to having university faculty and their students work directly with K–12 students. Faculty who want to field-test their ideas are naturally inclined to bring their students to schools to see if their ideas work. For example, a science educator focused on the travel patterns of butterflies brought his students to a fourth-grade classroom to have them each work with a fourth grader on tracking the travel of a specific butterfly.

Help With Administrative Staffing Needs

In addition to helping with professional development and student achievement, school–university partnerships help with administrative staffing needs. A favorite example is the outreach of Lenora Boehlert in Box 6.2.

University faculty and students can be an asset in providing workshops for parents as well. In one school–university partnership, a principal was quite frustrated because she did not know how to communicate in Spanish to non-English-speaking parents of students

Box 6.2   From the Assistant Superintendent's Desk on Help With Administrative Staffing Needs

Upon assuming her new position in a changing suburban school district, Assistant Superintendent Lenora Boehlert discovered that the schools in her district could not find decent substitute teachers. She knew that her predecessor had a good relationship with Manhattanville College's field-placement director and contacted her to see if this director could help her identify teacher candidates who might want to serve as substitute teachers. The college's field-placement director saw this as an opportunity to get more student teachers into the district. Together, they created a partnership that involved providing substitute teachers as interns, identifying schools to receive student teachers, and establishing a PDS with one of the elementary schools. Lenora came to the college to give workshops on the benefits of substitute teaching and identified a group of students who helped solve her substitute teaching dilemma.

at her school. She brought in a faculty-student team, both fluent Spanish speakers, to do a series of workshops for parents on ways to interact with the school. Another principal used student teachers to provide workshops to parents, again in Spanish, about the school's curriculum.

When school–university partnerships exist, there usually is a university liaison assigned to the school to be at the school a minimum number of days and/or hours per week. Such liaisons can assist principals, vice principals, and department chairs with a variety of instructional and administrative tasks. Liaisons, who essentially become members of the school staff (Rothstein, 2001), can weave in and out of classrooms to help school administrators identify classroom needs. They can help with the scheduling of events, the acquisition of resources, the development of projects, and the coordination of activities for students and professional development events for teachers. They can become a principal's unofficial assistant in identifying needs and proposing solutions for the school. When used well, liaisons are a great asset to principals for helping with administrative needs.

Challenges With School–University Collaborations

As might be expected, there are challenges to forming school–university partnerships, as described below.

Institutional Culture Clashes

An institutional culture clash speaks to a set of differing principles that different groups use to operate, for example, how one's day is scheduled, how one is compensated for one's work, how one is evaluated for job performance, how one's work environment should be managed, and how one defines professional development. Institutional culture clashes are particularly obvious between the K–12 and higher-education worlds, especially as school–university partnerships are formed. Classroom teachers are directly involved with their students most of the day. They use the end of the school day to catch up on the day's events, review student work, and prepare for the next day. They are not necessarily psyched for someone outside their immediate environment to tell them what or how to do their business. University faculty spend their days differently, with less time interacting with students and more time involved in committee work and scholarship that contribute to their understanding of specific academic disciplines. Their daily pressures are different, creating a different set of expectations for themselves and others (Wepner et al., 2008).

It is important to recognize institutional differences and help those within each type of organization come to acknowledge, appreciate, and work within and around each other's operational habits. A mix of communication methods such as face-to-face meetings, telephone conversations, printed material, and electronic tools can help (Wepner, 2011).

Communication

Usually we go up, down, and across within our own organizational structures. With partnerships, it is difficult to keep channels of communication open: A principal speaks with a dean about plans that include university faculty, yet fails to let his or her teachers know, or a dean fails to let faculty know. Teachers don't have time to speak with faculty, and plans go awry. One example is with a forensics lesson that was part of the cross-curricular learning experience (described earlier in the chapter). The science lesson, through forensic exploration, included biology students who actually helped the biology faculty member with the lesson. The biology students used the board game *Clue* as the basis for helping fifth graders understand how to formulate and test hypotheses by using fingerprinting, hair and fiber analysis, and blood samples to determine "whodunit." The biology students set up three learning stations so that each of the three groups of fifth-grade students could rotate to each station to use clues about the six suspects, six murder weapons, and nine rooms to solve the mystery of who and what killed Mr. Boddy and where it happened.

It just so happens that the first class of fifth-grade students that the biology students taught included special education students from a self-contained classroom. While enthusiastic for the project, the special education students did not respond appropriately to their guests. They made comments about the undergraduate students' physical characteristics. As a result, the undergraduate students did not want to return because they did not understand that these were special education students who had difficulty in knowing how to respond to new learning situations. The principal had not explained this scheduling configuration to the university professor or the project coordinator. As soon as the principal heard about this, she met with the entire fifth-grade team to establish expectations and alleviate behavioral problems; however, the damage already had been done (Wepner et al., 2008).

A linear organizational structure is supplemented with a cross-institutional system with many more voices in decision making. Educational leaders need to be aware of this change in the way communication occurs so that they can do their best to anticipate and stop potential problems.

Conflicting Expectations

Assumptions are often made that both the university faculty and school-based faculty want the same thing, but that is often not the case. For example, when university faculty go to a school to work with children, they might expect that the classroom teachers will work alongside them to learn about a specific instructional methodology and assist students with specific tasks. Classroom teachers, on the other hand, might see this as an opportunity to catch up on paperwork. Or, when university faculty come to a classroom, they might expect that the classroom teacher will reorganize the classroom, including seating arrangements, to accommodate a specific project. Classroom teachers, on the other hand, might expect that the faculty member will work within the existing physical layout of the classroom. Obviously, everyone needs to be explicit on what is expected.

Paradigm Shift

Developing a school–university partnership involves a paradigm shift about who is in charge and what is expected, especially as two different cultures are brought together. Superintendents and their central office administrators need to support both administratively and financially the work taking place in the schools. Principals need to initiate and sustain teamwork. They need to be interested in working with the college, able to convince faculty and supervisors of the value of such work, and willing to assume additional responsibilities to implement new ideas. Also important is the willingness of the college faculty to suspend typical teacher–scholar pursuits to work in the school. Classroom teachers need to be involved from the beginning in developing school–college projects. Otherwise, there will be subtle and not-so-subtle forms of resistance. Principals and education deans (or department chairs) need to be copartners who are intent on bringing together four different types of groups—classroom teachers, university faculty, K–12 students, and university students—to experiment with new types of learning experiences, provide professional development opportunities for teachers and faculty, and involve the next generation of teachers in the classroom to provide assistance as well as learn how to best promote student engagement.

One-Way Flow of Activities From University to K–12 Schools

Partnerships often originate from higher-education institutions and have faculty and their students going into a school or several schools to help with the curriculum, instruction, or assessment. A major concern from K–12 partners is a one-way flow of activities from the university to classrooms with little reason for teachers to take ownership of a project or to consider using the activities that have been developed by others not directly involved with the curriculum (Tomanek, 2005). Little regard seems to be given to what the teachers in the classroom want and need. As a result, the services offered by a university do not last longer than the time that university faculty and students are in a school. Partnerships are not sustained because there usually is a mismatch between the professional practices of the university faculty and the K–12 teachers, and time has not been devoted to developing a culture of professional learning and improvement. There also is not enough consideration given to K–12 teachers' demands on their time, especially within the current climate of accountability and high-stakes assessments (Moreno, 2005). Universities that create partnerships with K–12 schools need to be acutely aware of how to develop projects and programs that come from the teachers (Wepner, 2011). In other words, projects that are developed should come from teachers' recommendations. For example, as a result of the new Common Core State Standards, a team of middle school teachers might discover the need for help with those students who cannot read and respond accurately to reading passages. Teachers should be able to use a partnership to get such help and not have to worry about pet projects of university faculty that are unrelated to teachers' current needs. The CSI attempts to respond to teachers' needs.

Guidelines for Forming School–University Partnerships

Since there is very little downside to the forming a school–university partnership, what should educational leaders do to begin and sustain such opportunities? The following vignette of Marguerite Clarkson, a principal of a newly developed PDS, can provide ideas for getting started.

Marguerite became a new principal of an intermediate school (grades 4–6) in a changing suburban school district that experienced a large influx of non-English-speaking Hispanic students; this change created concerns among the teaching staff. Although she was an experienced administrator who had worked with the most challenging students in the past, she was not quite sure what to do to help these immigrant students and their parents assimilate into the school. Because her district was one of the districts invited to join Manhattanville's CSI Consortium, she decided to attend one of the meetings, where she learned about a Newcomer's Center that had begun in another CSI district to help Hispanic parents get acclimated to the school district. After the consortium meeting, she met with the director of the Newcomer's Center to arrange a visit. Once there, she realized that with support from her superintendent she could bring the Newcomer Center idea to her school. Within a year, she had done so and saw dramatic changes in the way that Hispanic parents were working with the school to help their children function and succeed.

At the CSI Consortium meetings, Marguerite also learned about the formation of PDSs in CSI districts. She thought that a PDS could help her implement certain needed programs and foster professional development among her teaching staff. She arranged to have her vice principal and lead teachers visit the oldest PDS in the network to see what was really happening. Her staff came back so exhilarated from the visitation that she immediately began the process of working with her assistant superintendent, superintendent, and Shelley to develop a partnership agreement. Marguerite and Shelley worked with their respective institutions to commit about $5,000 so the college would pay *for the PDS liaison and the school district would pay for PDS initiatives. Once they were both successful, a written agreement was signed.*

Marguerite worked with Shelley and other staff to identify a PDS liaison. She found space for the PDS liaison, who would spend two days each week working with teachers and students and supervising student teachers. She formed a PDS leadership team comprising herself, the vice principal, lead teachers, classroom teachers, and the PDS liaison. Together, they formulated goals for the PDS in line with school needs and set out to figure out a plan for accomplishing the goals. Marguerite, her PDS liaison, and her staff organized and hosted a memorable ribbon-cutting ceremony as a symbolic gesture of the official beginning of the PDS. This event, which was covered by the media, involved the entire school, central administration, the school board, and community leaders. Today, Marguerite's teachers are actively involved in some PDS initiatives, including data collection for their literacy program. Her students are involved in both during-school and after-school programs. She continues to go to the college for every CSI event and brings members of her staff and central administration to participate.

Marguerite began her journey by attending events at the college that led her to take ideas back to her own school and district. She and her staff actually visited an existing PDS to see whether it fit with their vision for their school. Once she saw excitement from her own staff, she enthusiastically and actively pursued the PDS concept with her administration and reached out to the college administration to develop a partnership agreement. She took the initiative to hire and work with her PDS liaison, form a leadership team of which she was a member, and establish goals for teachers and students that were appropriate for them. She also brought positive attention to her PDS so that she would have support from her entire community.

As Marguerite reminds us, a PDS is as strong as the school's leader. Peel et al. (2002) explain that a school-based leader is essential for the formation of clear goals, open lines of communication, and shared responsibility. Whether initiated by a superintendent, a principal, an assistant principal, a university administrator, or a faculty member, a

Guidelines for Forming School–University Partnerships

- Put liaisons in place
- Ensure communication among the stakeholders
- Have written agreements
- Make sure funding is available
- Assess partnership viability

PDS must have a principal who is committed to a PDS model, shepherding his or her staff to participate side-by-side with university faculty and students, and making time to communicate with key stakeholders so that the school can change accordingly. In addition to a strong principal, other factors contribute to a PDS's success.

Put Liaisons in Place

Because college faculty and classroom teachers are working together across institutional lines, they need to be able to go to representatives outside their own structures. A liaison needs to be in place at both institutions to solicit and communicate expectations and address the details of implementation so that the goals of a partnership are accomplished. While administrators (principals and education deans) might have the best of intentions for serving in these roles, they usually cannot devote the kind of time needed to satisfy all parties. School-based liaisons need to be given release time from teaching or other administrative tasks, free college coursework, or administrative stipends as compensation for this additional work.

Ensure Communication Among Stakeholders

A partnership requires frequent and productive communication among stakeholders so that participants have the same clear understanding of the partnership's purpose and function (Clark, 1999). Two considerations include the assurance of a two-way flow of communication and the inclusion of a variety of types of communication.

Two-way flow of communication. As explained earlier, too often a university initiates and controls the types of partnership activities that take place. It is imperative that teachers be involved in working with the university to determine projects so that there is mutual agreement on what will occur. For example, a third-grade teacher in a partnership school expressed concern to her PDS leadership team that she and her other third-grade colleagues needed help in implementing the new math series. The leadership team quickly figured out a way to bring a mathematics education faculty member and her students to the third-grade classrooms to help them implement the series. The mathematics education faculty member worked with the teachers on deciphering the new series' expectations, conducted demonstration lessons of some of the newer instructional methodologies, and cotaught lessons with the teachers. The university students worked with the students in small groups and individually on some of the more challenging math problems. The third-grade teachers were motivated to receive the university faculty and students in their classroom because they could observe and critique the use of new strategies with their students and have more time to observe their own students' responses to different strategies. Dyson (1999) explains that the most important outcome for a partnership is that it meets teachers' needs for their own program development.

Type of communication. Liaisons need to help those within each type of organization come to acknowledge, appreciate, and work within and around each other's operational habits. A mix of communication methods such as face-to-face meetings, telephone conversations, printed material, and electronic tools are suggested. Liaisons need to determine the tolerance level for each type of communication. If they find that face-to-face meetings yield disappointing rates of attendance, they should use the telephone and e-mail to communicate. Relevant e-mail distribution lists can help to disseminate information. A website for participants can be helpful if someone ensures that the website is current and relevant. If they find that their group thrives on face-to-face meetings because of the social networking opportunities, they should capitalize on this communication method. The method used is not as important as ensuring that communication exists so that partners can move toward common goals and meet the partnership's mission (Wepner, 2011).

Have Written Agreements

Written agreements are very useful because they lay out the purpose of the partnership, the roles and responsibilities of partners, any financial arrangements, and the intended duration. A written agreement can help alleviate the impact of leadership turnover, a problem that is not uncommon in any kind of partnership, because the agreement serves as a formal document of what the partners agreed to accomplish and contribute to the partnership. Signatures of the chief executive officers from each institution need to be part of the agreement to ensure official approval of the partnership (Byrd & McIntyre, 2011; Clark, 1999). Legal review and development of the written agreement help the chief executive officers and their boards to more readily endorse the language used in the agreement.

Establish roles and responsibilities of partners. A school–university partnership can be thought of as a marriage between the ivory tower and the real world. A school–university partnership is as easily break-able as a marriage between two people (School–College Joint Efforts Said to Remain Elusive, 1989) if equal partnerships between universi-ties and schools are not formed. Learning to reconcile differences between these two worlds must be dealt with from the beginning of the partnership by delineating roles and responsibilities of the people involved (Byrd & McIntyre, 2011; Duffield & Cates, 2008). Much of this is based on the initiators, purpose, and complexity of the partner-ship. For example, if a superintendent initiates a partnership, those involved would be different than if university faculty initiates. Those who initiate need to determine what needs to be done to be able to identify who should be involved, the responsibilities of those involved, and the duration of such responsibilities. There also needs to be an understanding that as partnerships evolve so will the num-ber of people involved. Take CSI for example. It began with one com-mittee of three faculty members and three administrators and evolved into five coordinating committees—each with different com-binations of university faculty, university administrators, school-based administrators, school-based faculty, and community representatives—and eight school-based committees—made up of school-based teachers, school-based administrators, university fac-ulty, and university administrators. Roles and responsibilities vary, based on the goals of an initiative or school and the tasks to be accom-plished. For example, in a middle school PDS, a director of the dis-trict's teacher center is working alongside the principal to initiate and implement projects. One school has its lead teachers on the leader-ship team. Another, because of the English language learner focus, has dual language teachers on the team. Those in charge simply need to be clear and open to change, making sure that those involved have appropriate assignments and are successful with accomplishing such assignments.

Make Sure Funding Is Available

Funding for partnership work needs to be adequate enough to support the partnership's mission. Everyone has limited funds. Grants can help, but they usually are temporary. Partnerships need long-term funding sources. Those who initiate partnerships need to figure out ways to reallocate funds, including the use of a barter sys-tem. For example, a principal in need of resources from the university offers her own services as a speaker for different university-based symposia as a way of saying thank you. A university faculty member provides workshops for parents at a school in exchange for using space in a building for her class.

Assess Partnership Viability

Because accountability is at the forefront of many of today's educational innovations, it is important to produce the evidence that partnerships are improving the knowledge and skills of teachers, teacher candidates, and K–12 students. This evidence must include data that can be shared with the larger educational community, school boards, media, and policymakers if school–university partnerships expect to receive the needed support (Byrd & McIntyre, 2011). A growing number of studies are supporting the assertion that school–university partnerships have great promise. For example, the Houston Consortium found that approximately 43 percent of teacher candidates believed they taught differently as a result of their participation in the partnership, made higher achievement scores on the state certification exam than a comparison group, and saw the achievement on the state-mandated achievement test of pre-K through grade 12 pupils increase after their schools became part of the consortium (Houston et al., 1999). Qualitative and quantitative assessments of both specific initiatives and the overall partnership should be conducted. Both school leaders and partnership participants should decide what and who is assessed and how (Willis, 2011).

Host big-ticket events and provide publicity. Big-ticket events contribute to promoting the partnership's viability and provide visibility for others about the importance of the partnership. Such events include conferences, symposia, ribbon-cutting ceremonies, dinners, luncheons, receptions, and award ceremonies. These events honor and celebrate the partnership and those who have had direct and indirect involvement. Formal ribbon-cutting ceremonies for every new PDS bring attention to their importance, especially when the superintendent and college president speak and jointly cut the ribbon. Conferences that include keynote speakers to set the tone and workshops to showcase the accomplishments of individual partners publicize the many positive and complex facets of partnerships. Award ceremonies help bring attention to those who have had the most impact on growing a partnership.

Big-ticket events are symbolic gestures that generate positive feelings toward those responsible for the work and financial resources. These events also help those on the periphery or in opposition to be more supportive of an institution's decision to donate personnel and material resources to such an initiative. Use of publicity and/or the media to cover such events can help generate even more excitement.

Concluding Remarks

The idea of school–university partnerships is not a new concept, yet it is currently recognized for its value by legislators, community leaders, corporate sponsors, and state departments of education. In a sense, school–university partnerships continue to be a coming-of-age story that brings together people, likely or unlikely, for the purpose of making something good even better. Partnerships require that someone take the lead in reaching out to the other institution. If the university has not yet reached out, superintendents, principals, or other designees already involved with the university should contact education deans, directors, chairpersons, or faculty. Partnerships require a *quid pro quo* in that each partner needs to give in order to get something in return. Partnerships require mutual respect from both university and K–12 schools in that whatever is accomplished is done with recognition of the needs of both parties. Partnerships also require leadership such that they have a fighting chance of moving forward. Those leading a PDS must, as Lee Iacocca (2007) said, pick the right people to participate and must set the right priorities. If there are leadership, respect, and give-and-take, partnerships have unlimited potential for transforming teachers and schools, helping prepare the next generation of teachers, and impacting student achievement.

7

Creating an Elementary Community School

For the newly appointed principal, the knock on the door from a local college professor was the catalyst that helped her transform her school from a low-performing school into a beacon of hope for children and families. In 1996, with the appointment of a new principal, the Thomas A. Edison School began the process of school reform when a college professor interested in working with a diverse student population approached her to offer his help. Having worked with English language learners (ELLs) in a variety of settings, the college professor hoped the school would benefit from his expertise. Coincidentally, at the time of their initial meeting, the principal was beginning to investigate ways to turn this low-performing school around. The college professor joined the school's advisory committee and began to channel college resources into the school. This suburban elementary school, located in a small town thirty miles north of New York City, is surrounded by some of the most affluent communities in Westchester County; however, during the past two decades it has experienced significant shifts in student demographics, including cultural, linguistic, and economic diversity. Similar to other suburban schools nationwide, this elementary school typifies the changes in suburban schools.

Description of School History

Prior to the arrival of the new principal in 1996, the Thomas A. Edison School experienced a significant shift in student demographics. Once a blue-collar working-class community, it had become populated with poor immigrant Hispanic families and was overcome by high levels of poverty, students with limited English proficiency, and frequent student mobility. In addition to these poverty-related issues, only 19 percent of fourth graders were passing state assessments. Furthermore, the school struggled with low levels of parental involvement because of parents' undocumented status and their beliefs that they should not take an active role in their children's education. Many undocumented and non-English-speaking parents facing difficulties of acculturation are often limited from participating in their child's education (Ferrara & Santiago, 2007). In her work with immigrant families, Dabbah (2006) describes how many recent arrivals to the United States often allow their own school experiences to shape their expectations of public schools; the perceptions of schools as an intimidating system inhibit parents from fully engaging in the educational process, which over time impedes children's learning.

The first step the principal took to address the myriad of issues faced by students and their families was to establish ongoing dialogues with parents, teachers, and members of the community. It quickly became apparent to the principal and the teachers that many of the families faced multiple levels of stress related to conditions of poverty and immigration and required a comprehensive social service delivery model at the school site to meet these needs. For children and families living in poverty, it often means limited access to health care, adequate nutrition, and the attainment of social-emotional, physical, and intellectual health. In an effort to create a school culture where children's overall well-being is considered as important as their academic success, an approach was used that garnered the resources of the community to transform itself into a hub of programs and social services for children and families.

Definition of Community School

The notion of a school as a centralized hub of resources for the community has its roots in the settlement-house movement. The settlement houses of the late 19th century were initially created by wealthy members of society as a social reform effort to improve the quality of life for poor, immigrant workers living in poverty-stricken areas (The

History of Settlement Houses, n.d.). These establishments became the nucleus of the community and a safe haven where housing, health care, education, and employment opportunities were made readily available for families lacking access to basic care. These forward-thinking institutions for social change were the precursor of today's community schools, creating the ideological context in which community schools currently operate (Dryfoos, 1998; Santiago, Ferrara, & Quinn, in press).

Purpose and Elements

Community schools, as defined by the Children's Aid Society (2001), are public schools that combine the best quality educational practices with vital health and social services offered at the school site to ensure that children are prepared to learn. The U.S. Department of Education further extends this definition:

> A community school is both a place and set of partnerships between school and other community resources. It provides academics, health, and social services, youth and community development, and community engagement and brings together many partners to offer a range of support and opportunities for children, youth, families, and communities. (U.S. Department of Education, 2009, p. 29)

By addressing the physical, social, and emotional needs through site-based services along with the cognitive needs met in the classroom, community schools emerge as a comprehensive approach to schooling that goes beyond a sole focus on academic achievement to include a more holistic approach to learning. As hubs of social services for the community with extended hours open before, during, and after the typical school day ends, community schools offer a range of programs to children and their families. Examples include but are not limited to youth development programs, enrichment programs, the arts, summer camps, medical, dental, mental and health services, adult education classes, immigration help, employment opportunities, or any service that addressees a community need. Because community schools are based on individual school needs, they differ in composition of services but maintain the same philosophical focus on community empowerment, coupled with positive educational outcomes for children.

It is no surprise that community schools transform traditional schools into new institutions (Children's Aid Society, 2001). However, transforming schools into new institutions requires a willingness to embrace a vision for education that includes partners as vital supporters of the work that takes place beyond the walls of the classroom. Embedded within the philosophy of community schools is a belief that partners work together to achieve a common goal, share responsibilities, collaborate, involve parents, and create comprehensive and integrated school-based services.

Examples of Community Schools

There are approximately 5,000 community schools nationwide according to Jane Quinn, the Assistant Executive Director for Community Schools (J. Quinn, personal communication, June 9, 2011). In their recent publication, *Financing Community Schools: Leveraging Resources to Support Student Success*, the Coalition for Community Schools indicates that schools nationwide at varying stages of development are committed to creating environments where students thrive and communities are transformed (Blank, Jacobson, Melaville, & Pearson, 2011). This movement now has the potential to grow exponentially with recent federal funding sources such as Race to the Top, Title I, and school improvement grants, thereby building systems that may greatly impact how public schools operate within the next five years. Although community schools share a universal commitment to a comprehensive and holistic approach to learning and family empowerment, they differ in both design and partnership resources. Some are considered full-service, meaning all of the partners are co-located at the school site, while others have off-site satellite offices for children and families to access the services. Regardless of which model is chosen, the mission and the message are the same: Comprehensive and integrative services delivered through partnerships are essential for children's overall well-being and academic success.

Some community schools are created using a broader system-wide approach. Approximately ten states have implemented systems; for example, in Oregon, Oklahoma, and Illinois, nonprofits, elected officials, corporations, philanthropists, and community members have joined together to develop and sustain community schools. This systemwide approach ensures that infrastructures are in place to support all components of the model, from the practical aspects of aligning services and defining partner roles and responsibilities to maintaining the integrity by keeping the vision and mission alive. Since 1999, the Schools Uniting Neighborhoods (SUN) Community School System in Multnomah County, Oregon, has effectively launched a districtwide model with at least 62 of its 150 schools becoming community schools serving 17,000 students annually. Each school within the network is assigned a site manager to coordinate all initiatives with the partner agencies, while partners and district personnel serve on the SUN Service Coordinating Council, which acts as a planning, monitoring, and governing body. Individual schools are responsible for maintaining site-based councils that respond to needs and oversee programs (Schools Uniting Neighborhoods, 2003). Oregon has been one of several states to build a systemic vision for community schools. The forward thinking on the part of district and government leaders certainly has the potential to guide other states interested in a new vision of schooling based on systemic change.

The Netter Center for Community Partnerships at the University of Pennsylvania sponsors the University-Assisted Community Schools network, which provides resources from its academic departments to support schools in the West Philadelphia area (Netter Center for Community Partnerships, n.d.). This long-standing partnership between the Philadelphia School District and the University of Pennsylvania is yet another example of a partnership focused on forward thinking and change.

Whereas some states elect to embrace a districtwide community school model, in New York City the public schools partnered with the Children's Aid Society to bring resources to some of their impoverished sites. Beginning in 1992, under the leadership of Children's Aid Society, nine New York City public schools became community schools. Children's Aid has maintained a solid partnership by providing various technical assistance support for both school design and operation and successfully helped bring cultural and community organizations, including universities, hospitals, and even Broadway theater companies, into the schools (Children's Aid Society, 2001). Public School number five on Manhattan's Westside is one of many Children's Aid sponsored schools; over the years it partnered with several cultural and community organizations, including the New York City Restoration Project, Broadway Theater Institute, Whitney Museum, Symphony Space, Riverbank, New York City Opera, Joyce Theater, and Touro College to actualize its mission (New York City Department of Education, 2011).

It is quite possible to create a community school using a grassroots approach as a stand-alone model in a district functioning autonomously rather than implementing districtwide or statewide initiatives. The stand-alone model, sometimes referred to as the *boutique style* community school, such as the Edison School, began with a grassroots approach spearheaded by the principal, based on the needs of her student population as well as the availability and willingness of community partners to combine their resources for a common goal. Incremental steps were taken during a three-year period to cultivate partner relationships before finally achieving a community school status. Today, after thirteen years, the Edison School continues its community school mission to provide comprehensive and integrative services for children and families.

Transforming One School

Principal's Analysis

To fully understand the transformative process that took place at Edison, it is important to examine the culture of leadership existing in most public schools prior to the standards and accountability movement of the mid-1990s. The leadership style at this time reflected a top-down approach with its historical roots grounded in the factory model of the early 20th century. In this model, the principal's role was defined by the ability to manage the organization rather than provide an educational vision for schooling. Edison School, like many others, mirrored the industrialized factory model of the time.

The school was once considered a dumping ground for less-than-effective teachers or those who were simply waiting for retirement. Collaboration was virtually nonexistent among most teachers, with many working in isolation, and delivering instruction that was weak at best. Teachers were not provided with professional development opportunities to enhance or improve their practice and often craved a professionally nurturing working environment where they could share their gifts. A large part of the teachers' frustration was attributed to former principals who chose to reinforce the status quo rather demonstrate strong instructional leadership. The culture of the school was such that on any given day you would find the principal behind the office desk tending to job-related administrative duties. The leadership style was considered hands-off at best, which allowed teachers full autonomy with little or no accountability. Clearly this was a school in need of strong leadership and a new agenda.

The leadership and instruction were not the only cause for concern. The 100-year-old physical plant had fallen into some disrepair with dreary classrooms and hallways, making the school's already poor reputation worse. The principal's tiny office, separated from the main office without access to the school's lifeline—the secretary—was both a physical and symbolic reminder that the principal's presence and leadership were separate from daily school occurrences. Moreover, since the school was located in the lowest income area in the district, its student population consisted of mostly poor and primarily Hispanic immigrants. Students, many of them designated as ELLs, struggled academically and lacked the skills needed to become successful learners. Furthermore, the allocation of resources did not accommodate the host of problems they brought with them. Bilingual classes could not sufficiently service the large number of eligible students; therefore, more classroom teachers needed English as a second language (ESL) certification or at least training in ESL strategies in order to effectively deliver instruction. In addition to the bilingual and ESL concerns present at the time, many students were classified as needing special education services to supplement their learning. Only two special education teachers were assigned to the school with caseloads far outnumbering their ability to provide services. Assigning teaching assistants to classrooms with a large number of special needs students could have offered additional help, but these positions were nonexistent. To further compound an already difficult learning environment, the school lacked a computer lab and a designated school library to help its students. These factors contributed to a malaise that left its teachers and staff feeling overwhelmed and burdened by the many challenges in place that interfered with appropriately addressing their concerns.

Change Process

Institutional change often requires the forward thinking of a leader to mobilize the community to face its problems and then challenge it to commit to making the needed changes (Heifetz, 1994). As educational leaders, school principals are the cornerstone on which school improvement ultimately rests; it is their vision, skill, and sense of purpose that moves the organization in a new direction. As Roland Barth eloquently stated, "It is not the teachers, or the central office people, or the university people who are really causing schools to be the way they are or changing the way they might be. It is whoever lives in the principal's office" (Houts, 1976, p. 21).

Luckily for the Edison School, a new principal with a clear vision for school improvement was appointed in 1996. Having served as both a teacher in the New York City public school system and as an administrator in a diverse suburban school district, the new principal, Eileen Santiago, had firsthand knowledge of the challenges faced by students and teachers and a plan for improving teaching, learning, and the school's reputation within the community. Her first charge

> **Box 7.1   From the Principal's Desk on the Change Process**
>
> Principal Eileen Santiago quickly identified three critical needs: the need to retain and hire the best teachers, the need to improve student performance by enhancing teachers' skills and knowledge, and the need to secure additional resources for instructional and capital expenditures. Instinctively, she knew that in order to make these as well as any other significant changes she had to gain the trust of the teachers and the community by establishing herself as an instructional leader with the skills that could turn around the school.

was to assess all aspects of the school, ranging from the layout of its physical plant to climate and outside influences that were impacting student learning. (See her thoughts in Box 7.1.)

The first year was spent building relationships with all school stakeholders because the principal firmly believed that the education of the children was the responsibility of all constituents. Philosophically and personally committed to creating an environment where children's developmental needs were addressed in much the same way as their intellectual needs, the principal set out on a journey to find innovative ways to turn her vision into reality. Moreover, she wanted a school that was inviting for parents and the community with a physical plant and infrastructure to support rich learning experiences. As stated earlier in the opening vignette, her first partner appeared coincidentally as she began to formulate goals for the school. The college professor heard that the new principal was eager to engage the community in the life of the school and reached out to offer help. Given the college's long-standing tradition of service to the community, combined with the School of Education's commitment to work with local schools, a context was created for a thriving, mutually beneficial partnership.

Involvement of Community

A basic tenet underlying the community school philosophy is that programs and/or services are created to respond to a need raised by its members. Responding to needs was critical to the success of Edison School as a community school. Early and ongoing dialogues initiated by the principal with all school stakeholders ensured that their voices were heard and that the concerns expressed were honored. The most pressing concerns for parents were after-school child care, homework help, and their own inability to communicate in English. The majority of parents were employed as unskilled laborers or domestic help who often worked two or three jobs late into the evening. With limited or no resources for child care, they scrambled to find safe environments where their children could be cared for and receive help with homework that the parents could not provide because of their own low literacy skills or language barriers. In response to a need for child care, a partnership with a community organization was developed to provide after-school homework help to about thirty students in grades 3 through 5. To support this initial program, the partner received a small grant. Eventually, a larger state grant was obtained to expand the program to its current status, which included remediation, enrichment, and homework help for children in grades K through 5.

Similar concerns were raised by teachers who reported that children were unable to complete homework and, as a result, were not independent learners with appropriate literacy and critical thinking skills. Teachers were also frustrated with low levels of parent involvement in their child's education due to their inability to speak English or their beliefs in taking a nonparticipatory role in school. Perhaps most upsetting to the teachers were the children routinely coming to school sick without access to basic health care to prevent common illnesses. Once again, in response to this need, another partnership was formed. In this instance, a local nonprofit medical organization sponsored a satellite school-based health center at Edison. Over the years, the school-based health center has facilitated medical insurance and health care for 99 percent of the students while also providing wellness checkups, immunizations, and prescriptions.

The partnership with the college initiated more than a decade ago grew incrementally, beginning with the placement of student teachers. The professor who offered assistance in the early days of the principal's tenure opened the door for a long-standing relationship that evolved into the creation of a professional development school (PDS) partnership. After many years of successfully developing its programs to support the needs of the school and the college, this mature PDS model has been replicated countywide.

Today, Edison School maintains four strategic partnerships that support its mission to provide programs and services that address the needs of children, families, teachers, and administrators. Although each partnership is unique in its approach, they share a common goal to respond to needs by delivering services at the school site where the services are easily accessible and have the greatest impact.

Pursuit of Funding

Funding the community school often requires the ability to think outside the box and develop a creative plan to secure funds. In order to finance community school initiatives, both the principal and school district administrators should possess a thorough understanding of school and district allocations, fundraising, grant writing, and negotiating for the exchange of services among partners. Federal monies such as Title I, Title III, and Title IV can be used to fund some initiatives, while other programs will be funded directly from the partnership agreements. It is important to think about the types of programs partners bring and to strategically plan how each will work in tandem. Regardless of the funding sources or partner agreements, an imaginative approach that combines resources is necessary.

Fortunately for Edison, the principal had the skills required to think outside the box and understood funding sources and was able to secure a federal earmark grant of $250,000 to create a community school. She knew that in order to have a school where students and families would flourish, fundamental changes in operation were needed to support both academics and social services under one roof. Furthermore, the principal was willing to open the school to partners as vital participants in the change process. While the school was in the planning stage of its transformation into a community school, a matriarch in the community school movement was looking for a site in the county that was ripe for this type of work. She heard that the Edison School was beginning to show some partnership activity and immediately contacted a New York state senator to inquire about the possibility of securing funding for the school. The senator envisioned a school as a hub for social services that were linked to the school and would be available to support the constituents in her district. A local advocacy agency, Westchester Children's Association, was given the charge to select a school willing to implement site-based partnerships as an integral part of its mission. Once the appropriate site was selected, the agency was responsible for overseeing the grant and providing technical assistance and training for a two-year period. As part of the agency's training initiative, school staff attended workshops at the Harvard Collaborative to learn more about this community-based model of schooling. At this same time, the school was introduced to the Children's Aid Society and the Coalition for Community Schools. These two organizations are committed to furthering the work of community schools nationwide. Collectively, these agencies strongly supported the school through its infancy and then gradually released their responsibilities as the school became more adept in its role and had a clear understanding of the community school model.

Involvement of a College and University

The opening vignette briefly describes the early stages of the bond between the college and the school. From the initial knock on the door more than a decade ago to the present-day partnership, this bond has been built on trust, mutual respect, and, perhaps most important, the willingness of two individuals and their respective organizations to spearhead this initiative. The placement of a cohort of student teachers in the early phases of the partnership provided many opportunities for the college supervisor, who later became the PDS liaison, and the principal to share their philosophies about teaching and learning and to identify ways to better support their students and faculty. They began to work closely together, trusting each other enough to pool their resources and find creative approaches to meet their respective needs. Over time they built structures within their organizations that were directly related to the common goal of improving teaching and learning outcomes. Each structure that was put into place responded to a desire expressed by the teachers or a need identified from analysis of program data. To this day, responding to needs guides partnership initiatives and new program development.

Role of CSI in the School's Transformation

As the college's first PDS, Edison remains a model of success due in part to the multiple supports made available through CSI. While the school was redefining its role as a PDS within a community school framework, it sought the expertise and resources of CSI to enhance its capacity. For example, when the school was struggling to find instructional strategies to help its ELLs, teachers enrolled in an ESL certificate program offered at the college; when the teachers wanted enrichment for students, an on-site science course was held in their classrooms; when the principal was investigating a new approach to literacy instruction, a pilot program was sponsored; when teachers requested remedial help for at-risk students, both an after-school and during-school tutorial program were implemented; when Hispanic parents requested a forum to address their concerns, CSI created the

Parent Leadership Institute; and when teachers wanted to reach new heights in their professional growth, they collaborated with college faculty on research, cotaught methods courses, or coauthored articles. Each of these CSI initiatives helped transform Edison from a community school into a community school with a unique focus, a PDS.

Data to Support Efforts With CSI

The power of the CSI to develop initiatives that respond to partner needs can be clearly seen in the school data collected thus far. Classroom teachers and students have benefited directly from the number of activities sponsored over the years, either on the college campus or at the school site. A large part of the PDS relationship encourages classroom teachers to work closely with teacher candidates and the course professors. In this building, 27 percent of the teachers hosted site-based methods courses, providing a laboratory setting for teacher candidates to develop their skills; 60 percent of the teachers hosted both student teachers and fieldwork students; and 100 percent have participated in some type of PDS-related work.

More than 50 percent of the teachers attended college-sponsored workshops, while 30 percent have conducted workshops for college students and faculty. At least three quarters of the staff took advantage of the college offerings, which were helpful for ESL training and recruitment of bilingual teachers. In fact, the PDS relationship with the college has been so positive in helping to address teachers' needs that 37 percent of the staff received second master's degrees from the college, 31 percent are alumni with 100 percent achieving tenure, 33 percent received post–master certifications, 60 percent have taken college courses, 5 percent are involved in a specialized college-funded literary training and research project, and 10 percent are adjunct faculty. Moreover, the school's two administrators and one district-level administrator are enrolled in the college's educational leadership doctoral program.

Challenges in Transforming a School

Overcoming Roadblocks

Change in any organization—regardless of its orientation as a business, school, or nonprofit—usually encounters resistance from its constituents. Fear, often accompanied by lack of knowledge or an unwillingness to change, will require those in positions of authority to make their goals transparent and engage stakeholders to buy in. Fortunately the principal arrived at a school where the staff desired a radical change in practices and expressed a need for strong visionary leadership. Given their willingness to embrace a new way of doing things, many of the attitudinal barriers commonly associated with school change did not occur. The staff fully understood their role was essential in order to create the desired environment at the school and considered the change both refreshing and welcome. Prior to assuming the leadership role at Edison, the principal was trained in group process, group dynamics, and consensus building. She was masterful in creating conditions to support buy-in from the stakeholders so that any roadblocks that occurred along the way were related to the implementation of the model rather than convincing the stakeholders of its merit.

The rationale behind Edison's becoming a community school was based on the philosophy that community schools are a strategy for school improvement, and site-based programs help overcome many of the socioeconomic barriers to learning that impede student achievement. Early conversations among stakeholders focused on improving the school and the lives of the children. From the principal's perspective, five major concerns surfaced for school improvement that could help reduce some of the barriers to student learning. First, the school needed to improve its image within the community. Second, the school needed to hire, retain, and retrain the best staff, including bilingual teachers and appropriate support staff, to achieve the goals stated in the improvement plan. Third, the school needed to improve student performance by enhancing teachers' skills and knowledge. Fourth, the school needed to secure additional resources and staff. Finally, the school needed to effectively communicate its mission to the district's new central office leadership team. During its evolution into a community school, many of these challenges were overcome one by one. Addressing one challenge often served as a solution for another.

For many years the school was thought of as a place for *those kids,* the poor and newly arrived immigrants without the resources to successfully compete in the academic arena. Focus groups of parents, teachers, and partners identified ways to make the school environment more inviting. These dialogues led to the development of a comprehensive school improvement plan with clearly articulated goals and outcomes. As the principal and stakeholders addressed each concern, their vision for improving teaching and learning began to unfold with quality instruction as the front-runner for all new initiatives brought into the building. Embedded within the plan was a focus on character education as the central theme guiding all school programs. The character education principles helped turn Edison into the caring and inclusive learning community that it is today.

Working With Teachers

The principal had a vision of transforming the school into a professional learning community where teachers would thrive and grow. In order to turn her vision into a reality, the principal needed to enlist the cooperation of the teachers. The first step was to change the school culture. The principal immediately began to involve the teachers in planning sessions by creating small committees responsible for examining various sections of the school improvement plan. A teacher from each committee participated in the monthly Community School Advisory Board meetings with representatives from each of the partner organizations. These meetings had several purposes: to provide partner and committee updates, respond to the needs of the community, and develop new programs based on the needs of the school. In addition to these board meetings, cohorts of teachers were taken to workshops to learn about community schools or partner organizations, and upon returning to Edison, conducted turnkey training for the entire staff.

Gradually a culture of collaboration, openness, and collegiality began to emerge. Now, teachers are involved in creating school conditions that respond to both the academic and nonacademic needs of their students and seek the help of school partners to address their concerns. Teachers' active participation in the decision-making process serendipitously led them to take on leadership roles within the school, such as chairing committees, working with the PTA, or serving on partner organizations. These leadership roles also extend to the ongoing professional development that has become commonplace within this collaborative culture. Teachers received professional development on a variety of topics, including subject-specific strategies targeting the needs of ELLs, the principles of character education, and developmentally appropriate practices. As a follow-up to each professional development opportunity, teachers voluntarily participated in interclass visitations to observe colleagues implement a new strategy, or if they felt particularly skillful in a certain area, conducted a workshop for the entire staff or a small group. Over time, the role of teachers has changed from working in isolated classrooms without much interaction from peers to becoming part of a dynamic learning community.

Working With Parents and the Community

Critical to the success of a community school is the involvement of the parents and the community at large. Since community schools are the hub of social service activity for its members, they must use feedback and respond to the feedback with need-based programming held at the school site. Edison worked hard to create an environment where parents felt accepted and could comfortably express their concerns. As a Latina woman, the principal was sensitive to the struggles faced by non-English-speaking parents, many of them undocumented Hispanic immigrants with a school experience vastly different from that of their youngsters. Parents were invited to meetings conducted bilingually to explain how American schools worked but, more important, involved them in discussions concerning their hopes for their children, difficulties encountered adjusting to a new culture, or problems relating to the impact of poverty on their lives. School partners became the conduit for addressing parental concerns by providing them with access to site-based social services. Parent programs ran the gamut from help with immigration to learning English to preparing their children for state assessments. Many of the original programs remain in place but have been expanded to include a focus on parent empowerment.

Working With Students

From the very beginning, the school's mission that is posted on the bulletin board for its students has been a focus on building community from the inside out and the outside in. Fundamental to the mission has been the infusion of character development and character education with a focus on core values and community building as an integral part of all school programs. To fully integrate character development into daily life, students recite each morning Edison's core value character pledge. These core values are used as the cornerstone for most disciplinary actions. Teachers and staff will often refer to the core values when an infraction occurs. Schoolwide character education programs take place on a bimonthly basis in the form of buddy classes. An upper grade is paired with a lower grade for an entire year for these buddy classes, which serve to enhance social skills and improve skills in an academic area. Another way the school develops character is through student participation in a variety of service learning activities. Edison has made a conscious effort to have its kindergarten through fifth grade students fully understand character, community, and their role in a community school.

Description of the School Today

Edison has gone from a school that was once considered the least desirable within the district to one that has received local, state, and national recognition for its ability to successfully close the achievement gap for low-performing students. It has hosted several local, national, and international visitors interested in learning about community school implementation. It is known as a site for best practices within the community school arena; in fact, Eileen Santiago presents regularly at conferences about this topic and has helped shape community school policies here and abroad. Edison now is a vibrant and dynamic leaning environment that responds to the needs of the children, families, teachers, and public by forming alliances with local organizations to support its mission.

Since its inception as a community school, Edison has enlisted the help of its partners to bring their expertise into the building while simultaneously helping to broaden their reach beyond the boundaries of the immediate school neighborhood. With the help of the mental health partner, a therapeutic counselor and a caseworker are on-site to work in tandem to support students and families in crisis by providing counseling, identifying social services, and lending a sympathetic ear. The caseworker also conducts workshops and training for the general parent population on topics that are intended to provide empowerment and leadership skills. With the help of the after-school partner, the after-school program has expanded to currently serve at least 150 students daily from 3 p.m. to 6 p.m. with homework help and enrichment activities. This program has been a lifesaver for working parents who need a safe, supervised setting for their children to get additional academic help but also has enrichment opportunities that the parents are unable to provide.

The college partner, the community health partner, and the adult education partner have also been responsible for providing programs and services that benefit the children, the families, and the teachers. With the help of the college partner, the school was able to form a PDS partnership that has grown from an initial placement of a cohort of student teachers into a true learning laboratory where teacher candidates, practicing teachers, and college faculty come together to examine classroom teaching practices in an authentic school setting. With the help of the community health partner, the health clinic located at the school has managed to supply medical insurance for 99 percent of the children. As a site-based clinic, it dispenses immunizations and prescriptions and also provides well-care visits, asthma education, and immediate attention to childhood illness. Considering the impact that health and well-being have on children's learning, this partner's role has been critical to students' academic success. With the help of the adult education partner, the school has offered evening classes to facilitate parent empowerment and help parents acquire the skills needed to navigate the educational system or find employment. Edison truly exemplifies the creative use of partnerships to find solutions for the myriad of challenges that schools are often unable to solve independently. The school has become a place for diverse groups of professionals to come together to provide fresh ideas and garner resources for the common good of its students.

Teachers' Attitudes, Qualifications, and Classroom Practices

The culture of the school changed over time, as did the attitudes and practices of the teachers. With the school's new emphasis on academic excellence, accountability, and growth for classroom teachers, a renewed sense of professionalism became evident. The commitment to a professional school environment was due to a comprehensive school improvement plan tied to teachers' professional development, the principal's efforts to respond to teachers' needs, and the principal's willingness to forge a PDS relationship with the college to enhance teachers' skills, dispositions, and practices. As a result of these schoolwide efforts, teachers began to engage in staff development opportunities that used data collected from supervisory observations, needs assessments, subcommittee feedback, and faculty meetings. Teachers' professional development plans were aligned with the school improvement plan for teachers to learn more about Balanced Literacy instruction, writing instruction, differentiated instruction, problem solving in math, instructional technology, co-teaching and preparing for the administration of state assessments. An emphasis was also placed on providing strategies for helping teachers and staff engage students in activities that fostered Edison's core values. Since the principal strongly believed in job-embedded staff development, she was able to secure funds to hire consultants for the entire school. While the consultants' initial visits provided the groundwork, their follow-up visits and progress monitoring were critical for helping teachers correctly implement suggested models or respond to general concerns. In addition to the monthly consultant work, weekly grade-level meetings also provided teachers with opportunities to share their insights and develop their expertise in a given area. After several years of ongoing, clearly delineated staff development, a noticeable shift emerged in teachers' confidence and competence in the classroom, regardless of their years of experience or stages of development.

The PDS partnership provided another venue for job-embedded staff development. Whereas the initial professional development efforts were designed to expand teachers' knowledge of instructional strategies, the PDS was designed to strengthen these skills and provide teachers with a context in which to apply and share them. Opportunities included the supervision of student teachers, hosting on-site methods courses, mentoring first- and second-year teachers, teaching graduate courses, serving on college committees, participating in research studies, coauthoring publications, and presenting at conferences. The college also provided on-site graduate courses and an array of programs at discounted rates so that teachers could enroll in areas of interest beyond initial certification. As a result of engaging in these PDS activities, teachers were exposed to new venues both within the school and on the college campus to further supplement their professional growth. Most important, teachers were willing participants in the creation of a culture of openness and reflection that has helped shape their classroom practice while also serving to shape the practice of college professors and the teacher candidates in their charge.

Student Achievement Differences

Student achievement in a community school encompasses both the academic and nonacademic factors that are critical to school success. When evaluating students' success, community schools take a more comprehensive approach by examining multiple sources of student data that impact student learning, including school behavior, school attendance, access to health care and social services, positive peer and adult relationships, and an orientation toward learning (Children's Aid Society, 2001). Edison has paid close attention to these factors through the regular collection of data to inform school decisions and assist its partners in their delivery of services. Over the years, surveys, attendance records, focus groups, and end-of-year reports have served as primary data sources for measuring student success and the success of the community school programs. In its analysis of the data from 1999 forward, Edison has found positive outcomes related to nonacademic measures of student success. Data indicate student access to primary health care rose from 23 percent to 98 percent, student attendance rates remain steady at 94 percent, disciplinary referrals fell from 25 percent to 10 percent, and parent attendance at teacher conferences rose to over 90 percent. Moreover, 100 percent of the students interviewed reported feeling a positive connection to school and learning.

Edison has shown growth in student academic achievement for more than a decade. In 1999, the percentage of fourth graders passing the New York state English language arts assessment was 19 percent, compared to 75 percent in 2009. In that same year, the percentage passing the New York state mathematics assessment went from 66 percent on grade level to 84 percent. Edison continues to ensure that students' needs are met at both the academic and nonacademic levels.

Community Involvement

Edison School has truly become the heart of the community where the community eagerly awaits its annual traditions. The annual Gallery Walk replicates a museum setting where students showcase a thematic approach to learning, culminating in an evening of integrated arts. The Hispanic Heritage Day, sponsored by a community partner, shares cultural traditions and foods from students' native homelands. The Fashion Show and Edison's Catch a Rising Star are just two of the many fundraisers held at the school involving students and, at times, community partners. While helping raise money for the school, these events provide an evening of fun intended to build community participation that is vital to the life of the school.

Future Goals

Recently the school experienced a change in leadership with the retirement of its principal, but Edison hopes to continue its history as a community school under the leadership of its new principal. The former principal and the Community School Advisory Board carefully crafted plans for succession. The strategic action plan, along with a comprehensive partner manual describing the roles, responsibilities, and institutional mission, provided the new principal with a framework for understanding the complex nature of a community school. Edison's policies and procedures are firmly in place with a clearly articulated mission that guides the work of its partners and staff members within the building.

A focus on students' academic performance will remain at the center of all community school initiatives so that its partners continue to bring high-quality programs into the school. Having received state and national recognition for many years as a high-performing community school, Edison will continue its long-standing tradition of community engagement, academic rigor, and parent advocacy to improve the lives of children and their families.

Guidelines for Forming a Community School

Before school leaders consider the "musts" or "have-tos" of the community school guidelines listed below, it is important to bear in mind these practical suggestions for implementation. First, understand the community school model and its implications for practice. Second, be fully committed to working with partner organizations. Third, identify school needs and possible solutions. Fourth, align partner programs with the school's mission. Fifth, creatively use financial and human resources. Finally, start small and build on successes. Like any new initiative or undertaking, creating a community school requires those involved to think differently about their roles and the ways in which they conduct business.

Guidelines for Forming a Community School

- School leaders must embrace and promote the community school concept
- Teachers need to open their classrooms to community partners
- Partners need to support both the school and community

School Leaders Must Embrace and Promote the Community School Concept

The success of any organization is directly related to the ability of its leader to move the organization forward in both actualizing its mission and helping its constituents to actualize their own potential within the organization. The leader's ability to communicate effectively, work collaboratively, and build trust is necessary for organizational success. Community school principals must possess these qualities and so much more. First and foremost, the principal must have a clear understanding of the community school philosophy, and it must be embedded in the decision-making processes that guide the work of the school. Since community schools are fundamentally different from traditional schools, leaders must be able to work across the institutional boundaries of its partner organizations to understand their structure and the programs they bring to support the school. Moreover, these leaders must be able to think creatively about the sharing of building space to facilitate the co-location of agency partners, must be skillful negotiators, and must be able to help diverse groups of partners reach a consensus about school-related issues. Most important, these leaders must truly embrace a vision of schooling that involves the community in the daily life of the school.

Teachers Need to Open Their Classrooms to Community Partners

Teachers in community schools understand that, in order to meet the multiple challenges faced by their students, support is needed beyond what they can provide within the classroom. Therefore, the role of the teacher in a community school is one that combines classroom responsibilities with the ability to work collegially and collaboratively with partner agencies to support the overall well-being of students. When teachers willingly access the help of school partners, they no longer work in isolation or in silos typically associated with classrooms but are part of a professional learning community. Furthermore, teachers begin to view their roles as expanding outside the walls of the classroom to include interaction among community partners.

Partners Need to Support Both School and Community

In community schools, partners share a vision for education that looks beyond standardized test scores to include a more broadly defined goal of student success. Partners understand that their primary role is to support the needs of the school, while simultaneously supporting the needs of their respective organizations. By doing so, community partners set up reciprocal win-win relationships based on trust and mutual respect, which often results in opportunities for cross-boundary leadership to emerge. In these new leadership roles, partners with varied skill sets and professional orientations work collaboratively across prescribed institutional roles for the common goal of student success. When all members of the school community take responsibility for student outcomes, a can-do culture is born, community challenges are seen as opportunities for growth, and partners are seen as the mechanism for achieving success.

Concluding Remarks

As suburban schools begin to confront the significant shift in student demographics, the community school may emerge as one way to tackle the host of complex social issues often facing students. For more than a century, community schools have led the charge to provide basic care for students and families with services and programs held at school sites that address their intellectual, physical, social, and emotional needs. Those who work in community schools understand that factors beyond the classroom significantly influence student learning and ultimately impact students' success in life. When all members of the community truly share the belief that student learning is related to multiple factors beyond the classroom, then and only then can they build structures that support partners, programs, and a vision of schooling called the community school.

8

Working With Parents

Marta is a young parent and an immigrant. She had absolutely no idea about school programs or how to guide her son when the time came for him to attend school. Marta learned about an early literacy program at the elementary school in her community from Spanish flyers and school outreach in her neighborhood. She heard about the welcoming atmosphere at the school and how much the school's program helps Latino parents and children. Marta attended this early literacy program with her son and learned how to work with him to promote his literacy development. She also learned English language skills and learned more about her community. She made friends with other parents, many of whom were in her situation, and listened to their experiences with the schools. Marta wants to continue attending parent meetings and workshops at the school because she feels they are very important for helping to guide her son.

Parents play an integral role in their children's education. Parents set the standards and expectations for academic performance and influence educational goals. Schools realize the importance of involving parents in their children's education. There are, however, challenges for schools to appeal to the various groups of parents who represent different racial, cultural, socioeconomic, and educational backgrounds. Additional challenges for schools involve reaching out to parents who are lacking knowledge of English, navigating a new culture, and challenged by the expectations and standards of schools in the United States. These parents are uncertain about their role in their children's education.

As mentioned throughout the book, suburban school districts have been seeing increases in diversity among their students. It is important to identify and understand the various needs and issues of parents in changing suburban school districts in order to cultivate and maintain parent involvement.

This chapter discusses the needs and challenges that parents have, describes opportunities for schools to minimize these challenges, and provides ideas and guidelines for involving parents in various levels of partnership with the schools that ultimately promote student achievement.

The Importance of Parents as Partners in Children's Education

Parents are important in supporting their children's work in school and setting goals for their children's achievement. Involvement of parents in their children's education benefits school district personnel, the parents themselves, and their children.

In the changing suburbs of Westchester County, New York, Board of Education candidates made parental involvement in suburban school districts a major election platform. Incumbent Jerome Smith stated in *The Sound Report*, "Parents are important because that is who education begins with. When the child returns home [from school] they keep learning. It has to be a complete loop to be successful" (Maker, 2010, p. 3).

Parent involvement covers a range of activities such as attending school functions and meetings, helping children with homework, providing encouragement, providing a home environment that is conducive to study, modeling behavior such as reading, advocating for their children's education, and volunteering for activities at school.

The Impact of Parents on Student Achievement

Beyond the classroom, successful youngsters are more likely to engage in a well-rounded, balanced array of activities than are less successful youngsters. Deliberate out-of-school learning and work activities are a second major category of activity that provides opportunities for mental stimulation through cognitive work. (Clark, 1990, p. 5)

The most effective forms of parent involvement are those that engage parents in working directly with their children on learning activities at home. The earlier in a child's educational process parent involvement begins, the more powerful the effects (Cotton, 2000).

Students with parents who are involved in their school tend to have fewer behavioral problems and better academic performance and are more likely to complete secondary school than students whose parents are not involved in their school (Henderson & Berla, 1994). Parent involvement also has a direct influence on students' beliefs about their ability to complete schoolwork successfully, their motivation to learn, and their ability to set goals for themselves (Hoover-Dempsey & Sandler, 2005).

The Parent Institute for Quality Education (PIQE) is a national organization that creates partnerships between parents, students, and educators to further students' academic success. As a result of PIQE's work since 1987, more than 1.5 million underserved students have been helped (Valladolid, 2010). One of PIQE's guiding principles is that parents and teachers must work together to ensure the educational success of every child. PIQE's signature program is the Parent Education Program, which focuses on creating a bridge between home and school ("Parent Engagement Education Program," 2010). Longitudinal studies in California have followed children of parents who graduated from PIQE and found that most of the children go on to postsecondary education (Graham, 2010).

There is what is called a *curriculum of the home* that is an important determinant of learning. It includes informed parent–child conversations, discussions about reading, and interest in children's academic and personal growth (Walberg, 1984). Parental involvement has a measurable impact on students' achievement and future careers. For example, children with very interested parents progressed 15 to 17 percent more in mathematics and reading between ages 11 and 16 (*The Impact of Parental Involvement in Children's Education,* 2008). Parental activities that foster achievement of middle and secondary students typically include developing postsecondary plans, monitoring homework, working on coursework, and program planning (Cotton, 2000).

On the flip side, secondary student dropout rates are higher for children whose families are less involved in their education (Henderson & Berla, 1994). For example, Latino schooling in the

United States has long been characterized by high dropout rates and low college completion rates (KewalRamani, Gilbertson, Fox, & Provasnik, 2007). Latinos who are in middle school have a significant gap in reading and mathematics achievement, compared to their non-Hispanic white and Asian student counterparts (Lopez, 2009). Latino adults and youth identify the lack of parental involvement as a major reason for their achievement gap in school (Lopez, 2009). A survey conducted of 16- to 20-year-olds by Pew (Lopez, 2009) revealed that foreign-born Latinos are likely to blame their parents among other things for poor performance in school.

Student achievement improves when parents promote learning in the home environment, reinforce what is being taught at school, and develop the child's life skills. Student achievement also is helped when parents serve as advocates for their children in school and help their children receive fair treatment. Parental involvement and efforts to engage parents are critical issues for school leaders.

Issues of Parents in Changing Suburban School Districts

Parental beliefs and perceptions have been shown to be strong predictors of involvement. For example, middle-class families are willing to take collective action to gain access to schools and obtain resources (Lareau, 1989). In contrast, minority or low-income parents are often underrepresented among parents involved with schools (Cotton, 2000).

The Thomas Rivera Policy Institute (TRPI) held Hispanic parent focus groups and found that Hispanic parents identified the following barriers to parents' involvement in the schools (Zarante, 2007):

- Lack of education of the parents themselves
- Language limitations (no knowledge of English and lack of native-language literacy)
- Reluctance of parents to question authority (teachers and schools)
- Feeling intimidated by teachers
- Reluctance of parents to advocate for their children
- Infrequent, impersonal, and untimely communication from the school, with electronic postings to English-speaking parents only
- Difficulty reaching teachers by phone

- Perception that there needs to be a problem in order for parents to contact the schools
- Inability to understand school policies and legal rights
- Discrimination
- Lack of receptive and cordial atmosphere at school
- Deterred by security measures at school

Another factor found was Hispanic parents' hesitation to ask for time off from work for school activities because they feared losing their jobs with demanding and inflexible work schedules (Smith, Stern, & Shatrova, 2008). A discussion about the context that surrounds some of the above issues follows.

Cultural Differences

Many low-income Hispanic parents view the U.S. school system as "a bureaucracy governed by educated non-Hispanics whom they have no right to question" (Nicolau & Ramos, 1990, p. 13). As a result, parents are reluctant to question authority because they believe they are overstepping their boundaries and showing disrespect to the teacher (Smith et al., 2008).

Cultural differences also affect the way in which children respond in the classroom. Children from collective cultures who are used to sharing enter U.S. classrooms where students own things and operate for the good of the individual. This causes immigrant children to feel confused and isolated when facing this new behavior in a classroom group setting (Z. Tazi, personal communication, May 23, 2011).

Language

The lack of English language knowledge is a major barrier to school involvement for parents. When parents do not have adequate knowledge of the English language, they are not able to understand correspondence sent home from the school and teacher, school website information, information on school policies and forms, and all other school-related issues.

Parents who lack English skills cannot assist their children with homework, cannot read to their children in English, and cannot help them with other school-related activities related to academic success.

Parents are reluctant to approach school personnel due to their inability to communicate effectively in English. Parents who do not speak English (parents who did not learn English as a child and currently speak a non-English language in the home) are less likely than other parents to attend a general school meeting or school event or to volunteer or serve on a committee ("Parent Involvement in Schools," 2010). Parents are ultimately unable to advocate for their children.

Socioeconomic Status (SES)

Pedro Noguera (2007) said that few schools in affluent suburbs, where resources are abundant and poor and minority children are few in number, are effective at closing the racial achievement gap. He noted that the reason some schools succeed in closing or at least reducing the racial disparities in achievement has less to do with skill than will, that is, the dedication and commitment of educators and deliberateness of the approach they take in meeting the needs of the students they serve. Noguera (2007) added that one of the strategies that these effective schools have in place is the commitment to engage parents in education.

While some immigrant groups such as Asians tend to do well in academic and economic arenas, other groups, such as Hispanics, generally do not (Smith et al., 2008). Low-income parents typically are not involved in ways that schools expect and often fail to adequately access and benefit from school resources (Lareau, 1989).

Parent participation in education can be more predictive of students' academic success than family socioeconomic status (Walberg, 1984). Noguera (2007) points out that the beliefs of the educators determine whether gaps in achievement close and all children learn. "Children know when they are being taught by adults who care about them and who believe in them" (Noguera, 2007, p. 2).

Poverty

It is important to examine poverty and its impact on families and students because this is a growing and major consideration for schools. At least one-third of the nearly five million children of undocumented immigrant parents living in the United States are poor (Lopez, 2009). Hispanic immigrant children are likely to be poor, and the poverty rate for children from Hispanic families is higher than the poverty rates for children in other ethnic groups. "High child poverty rates persist among nonimmigrant Hispanic families" (Rector, 2006, p. 16) as well. Children's living conditions, combined with the work requirements of parents and children, create stress on parents and children, which impacts the children's schoolwork.

Zoila Tazi (personal communication, May 23, 2011), Principal of Park Early Childhood Center in Ossining, New York, identified poverty as a significant obstacle in parent engagement. The issues related to poverty are layered. It is not just a financial issue. Poverty impacts the experiences of children, the comprehensive needs of children, and the learning process for children. Zoila noted that poverty has a social and emotional impact on children as well. Children see things in school that they do not have at home and feel shame and fear.

Low education levels contribute to high levels of persistent poverty among nonimmigrant Hispanics. Zoila Tazi noted that generational poverty is another consideration as it passes from generation to generation in that the parents have needs, their children have more needs, and these needs escalate with each new generation.

School leaders must think broadly about poverty issues, and they must try a holistic approach in dealing with poverty issues. Schools must try to support students living in poverty on multiple fronts so that they have an opportunity for equitable outcomes in their education. Schools must ensure that children begin to develop the needed vocabulary to understand and read text and acquire habits that lead to their healthy development (Z. Tazi, personal communication, May 23, 2011).

Work Responsibilities

The pressure and demands for parents to work multiple jobs, often just barely supporting the family, prevents parents from having the needed time and focus to be involved in their children's school and homework. Parents fear that taking time off from work will result in the loss of their job. This results in time constraints to dedicate to their children's schoolwork or school meetings.

Family expectations and financial pressures place a different expectation or priority on education for some Hispanic youth. The biggest reason for the gap between the high value Latinos place on education and their modest expectations to finish college appears to come from financial pressure to support a family (Lopez, 2009).

Schools should be aware that a lack of involvement is not indicative of the level of commitment that parents have to their children. Generally speaking, parents have high goals for their children that are tied to academic achievement. Challenges generated by socioeconomic factors prevent parents from being involved for many reasons. Suburban school districts must identify and work with socioeconomic barriers in order to achieve meaningful and successful partnerships with parents (Smith et al., 2008).

Promoting Parent Engagement in Changing Suburban Schools

School and teacher practices are the strongest predictors of parental involvement (Dauber & Epstein, 1993). Specific practices that promote parental involvement include assigning homework designed to increase parent–student interaction, holding workshops for families, and communicating to parents about their children's education. Programs designed to foster linkages between families and schools help to compensate for limited family resources and effectively alter the traditional relationship between SES and school performance (Henderson & Berla, 1994).

This section describes the efforts of suburban school districts to promote parent involvement, how various school district personnel are addressing the needs of parents in light of the demographic changes in their schools, and how challenges have been minimized to reduce barriers for successful parent partnerships.

Interestingly, many of the school district personnel are immigrants themselves. They are bilingual (Spanish–English) and have the experience of and empathy for the immigration and assimilation process themselves. Richard Organisciak (personal communication, June 7, 2011), Superintendent of the New Rochelle School District in New York, New York, is an immigrant and has a soft spot for immigrants when they are dealing in a zone of discomfort.

All school district personnel involved in parent relationships agree that outreach, communication, and programs tailored to the parents' needs are critical for success. Parents need to be empowered, and the schools need to acknowledge and support whatever the needs and characteristics are.

Changing Suburban Schools' Approaches: Overcoming Challenges and Reducing Barriers to Parent Engagement

A school leader's orientation and philosophy influence the nature and scope of a parent partnership. An administrator can have a powerful impact on a school's culture that in turn impacts the efficacy of parent engagement efforts. (See Box 8.1 for reducing barriers to parent engagement.)

Schools with the most successful parent involvement programs are those that recognize that parents differ greatly in their willingness, ability, and available time for involvement and offer a variety of ways that parents can participate.

Box 8.1 From the Principal's Desk on Reducing Barriers to Parent Engagement

Zoila Tazi, Principal of Park Early Childhood Center in Ossining, New York, asserts that the school takes on responsibilities for the community and, therefore, must develop a culture of respect, support, and love. The school must communicate that it wants the same success that the parents want for their children. Parents then place an interest in their child's education, which then stimulates involvement. Zoila said that parents become so eager to collaborate with the school that they are undeterred by rain, sleet, or snow, similar to what is said about the post office. Once this culture has been communicated and established, it becomes easier for the school to figure out the additional needs. (Z. Tazi, personal communication, May 23, 2011)

As discussed in Chapter 7 and observed by Zoila, schools are increasingly becoming the central place where programs occur that address and meet the needs of parents. The school sets the tone for the community. Zoila adds that the school district needs to make the claim that it is focused on ensuring equitable outcomes for students and is providing opportunities for all segments of the population in the district. Zoila's school district, like many of the suburban school districts, has many diverse groups and many different issues and needs. She feels that school districts must cast the widest possible net to address parents' needs and that the needs of any particular group should not be underestimated.

The school district superintendent influences the culture of the district in promoting parent partnerships. Superintendent Organisciak, mentioned earlier, said, "Parent engagement is a political reality. A strong parent base does influence a school district. I will do whatever I can to strengthen parent voices." He said that parent input is designed to help their children do better and it would be foolish to ignore the input that is designed to help their children. (See Box. 8.2 for more on parent engagement.)

Outreach

Many suburban school districts have designed successful outreach efforts for parents. School district leaders have developed bilingual website information, bilingual communication and correspondence to parents, and information about bilingual social workers, community

Box 8.2   From a Community School Coordinator's Desk on Parent Engagement

Maria Flores, Community School Coordinator at the Thomas A. Edison School in Port Chester, New York, says that a major challenge is reaching parents who have two to three jobs and are struggling just to have enough food for their families. Information must be disseminated in a way that is easy to share in the neighborhoods and the community. Maria added that the schools also deal with the element of fear that parents have that comes from not having documented status. The schools must acknowledge their fears, demonstrate understanding for this key stressor, and "go the extra mile for parents by understanding their needs." (M. Flores, personal communication, June 8, 2011)

Box 8.3   From the Superintendent's Desk on Parent Outreach

As Superintendent, Richard Organisciak has set the goal for his district to make the schools an informative, nonthreatening, and welcoming environment for parents so that they are confident about interacting with the school district and they stay engaged. He points out that the first visit for the parent to the school should not be the first day of school. His schools reach out to parents during the summer by inviting them to informal social events. The schools conduct this outreach in the neighborhoods (churches, Laundromats, restaurants) to maximize visibility of event information for parents. Involved parents will engage other parents in the community. (R. Organisciak, personal communication, June 7, 2011)

school coordinators, and teachers who are empathetic and trustworthy. Many of the schools' outreach efforts extend far out into the community in order to reach as many parents as possible about school programs.

Richard's approach to parent outreach (see Box 8.3) is that he always wants parents to feel heard, understood, and valued. He feels strongly that parents need to be respected, especially when they have an issue with their child, so that they have the confidence to seek help and agree to the programs that their child needs. Parents need to find people at the school whom they trust. If the school provides such people, it then starts a good cycle of satisfaction and thus promotes continued engagement with the school. Richard works to break down institutional barriers by helping parents become comfortable in coming to school, returning for more programs, and thus engaging with the school. Collaborative partnerships with parents eliminate the dynamic that the schools are the "learned ones and you are the parents" (R. Organisciak, personal communication, June 7, 2011).

As mentioned in previous chapters, Newcomer Centers in some school districts and community organizations target immigrant families and offer programs for parents and children to help them assimilate. Newcomer Centers offer English language classes, a welcoming and nonthreatening atmosphere, and support for issues families face when relocating to the United States. Schools often partner with the community organization Newcomer Centers that have strong outreach to cultivate parent relationships.

Communication

Communication to parents from the schools should be in the parents' native language. This includes correspondence, website information, and meetings at school. In some schools, outreach case managers are the points of contact who reach out to parents in their native language. This is particularly critical when reaching out to parents who are new immigrants and/or do not speak English.

In the Thomas A. Edison School, the outreach case manager will address a multitude of needs for the parents and families, such as health care, forms, clothing, and the purchase of school supplies. The outreach case manager engages parents while supporting them in the assimilation process. By helping to meet a family's basic needs, the manager develops a relationship and trust is built, which helps promote support for all other school initiatives.

The accessibility of school district administrators is a powerful communication tool as it sends a positive message to the parent community. Many principals of suburban schools are available to parents and are present at parent programs. The accessibility of a superintendent sends a profound message to parents. Superintendent Organisciak's experience with two Latina mothers illustrates this point. Two Latina moms went to his office to try to get a response to the cancelation of an after-school program that taught English and computer skills to their children. He reinstated the program after hearing their needs and assessing other issues. This positive experience for parents quickly spread throughout the community and communicated his commitment to partnering with parents.

Before- and After-School Initiatives

Many suburban schools have been conducting programs and workshops for parents for several years. These programs are based on the needs of the parents and were developed by teachers, administrators, and outreach coordinators who understand and empathize with the challenges that parents face.

The Ossining School District has its First Steps program, which is an early childhood literacy program that starts with the child at birth and involves both parents and children. The program offers basic literacy skills to both parents and children and teaches the parents how to work with their children on literacy. Zoila Tazi said that the First Steps literacy program in the Ossining district is monitored, and results indicate that parent involvement does favorably impact achievement and participation in parent–teacher conferences.

The Ossining School District also works with a community organization on a parent outreach program called *Proyecto Alcance* that provides leadership, education, and advocacy for parents in after-school workshops.

The Thomas A. Edison School in Port Chester (see Chapter 7) uses specific programs for parent outreach and education. The Ready, Set, Go program has literacy-based components, which gives parents tools to support their children's literacy development at home. Parents are given strategies for reading aloud to their children and ideas for engaging their children in the text. The program also helps parents promote language development at home by discussing everyday habits such as getting dressed. The premise is that parents are the child's first teacher. Another parent program at this school is Every Person Influences Children (EPIC). This program is made up of seven to eight lessons and emphasizes that learning occurs everywhere. The program teaches parents how to reinforce learning with their children in daily activities, such as going to the supermarket or waiting in a doctor's office. *The Common Sense Parenting* by Boystown (n.d.) focuses on everyday discipline, provides structural ideas for use at home, and complements EPIC.

Additionally, as discussed in Chapter 3, the Thomas A. Edison School runs a parent discussion and education group called Second Cup of Coffee (*La Sugunda Taza de Café*) that meets on a weekly basis. Maria Flores from the Thomas A. Edison School said that once the parent is a partner with the school, it is easier to support the child's academic achievement (personal communication, June 8, 2011).

Teachers at schools often see a need for parent education and support and initiate after-school parent groups. Tina Guzzetti, a teacher in the New Rochelle School District at Webster Elementary School, started Parent University back in 2002. Tina saw an increase in immigrant students in her classroom and formed an after-school English class. Tina teaches a group of parents (and even grandparents!) English while the magnet facilitator works with the children on homework and enrichment activities. Several years ago, she incorporated one day of instruction for both parents and children in the school computer lab. Tina observed that this is a wonderful opportunity for participants to work at their own speed and level while focusing on their specific needs and interests. The classes are open to any family in the school district and cover not only English language skills but also school culture, computer skills, and how to prepare for U.S. citizenship. These classes provide parents with a safe place to learn English and, as a result, they share information about this program with other parents in their respective communities. Tina says that she is inspired by the power of parents and children learning side by side. Children see that parents are not just saying that school is important; they are demonstrating it through their actions.

The Parent University families form a strong community that provides individuals who often feel disenfranchised with a sense of belonging and purpose. Over time, the school principal, teachers, and staff have noticed a change in the parents' behavior from being apprehensive to feeling more comfortable with their surroundings at the school. The sense of pride and belonging has a positive effect on their children and on their children's academic performance. A testament to the success of this program is that students who participated at younger ages with their parents have come back to the program as middle school students to help. Tina said that she started this program because it was personally important for her to do this for her students and families (T. Guzzetti, personal communication, May 23, 2011).

Special Education Classifications, Services, Support, and Rights

Navigating the world of special education classifications and services is difficult for most parents, given their lack of familiarity with the concepts and forms. For non-English-speaking parents of children with special education needs, it is even more daunting. School administrators need to know how to help non-English-speaking parents navigate the special education evaluation process. There currently are a limited number of terms, definitions, and forms available in Spanish for parents of children with learning or behavior disabilities. Parents should know that their children are entitled to evaluations in their first language, and parents are entitled to translation services to get the appropriate arrangements made for their child (M. Malow, personal communication, June 13, 2011). Parents also need to know that their children might not need special services because they do not have learning problems; rather they need assistance in learning English.

Collaboration with higher education institutions can be a source of information for parents. The Changing Suburbs Institute (CSI) program organized workshops in Spanish for parents of special education students to provide basic information about special education terms and classifications and how to identify and help their children with these issues.

The Thomas A. Edison School also runs special education workshops for parents in their native language. These workshops promote parent engagement with the special education services provided for their children. Anecdotally, school personnel noted major changes in parent behavior and relationships once parents participated in these workshops.

Role of Higher Education: Leadership and Resources

Higher education institutions in general are in a perfect position to leverage their school district partnerships to bring programming for parents to another level. Higher education institutions are by nature able to cast a wide net in the community and involve many participants in developing influential programs.

The CSI program worked with its school district partners to assess the needs of the schools and parents. The college then involved key school personnel in the development and planning of a parent-education program that would enhance the schools' efforts. An important part of this program was the development of a leadership conference for parents from different communities across the suburbs to come together and work as a unified group. Zoila Tazi said that such a conference enables parents across districts to talk to and learn from each other, especially that they are not alone with their issues and challenges. The parents learn as much from each other as they do from the speakers and workshops.

Zoila said that the college partnership in general validates the efforts of the schools when a college makes the schools part of its mission. The schools value that they are part of something bigger. She added that an important approach of the college's programs is its mission to make change happen, especially when it comes to working with parents.

CSI's annual Hispanic Parents Leadership Institute resulted from school, higher-education, and community collaboration. The goals of this annual conference are to educate parents about the U.S. educational system and help them become leaders and advocates for their children's education. Funds for the conference come from local organizations. Invitations to parents are coordinated at the school level so that trusted and familiar faces at the schools ask parents to attend. The entire conference is held in Spanish and is composed of a keynote speaker and several workshops on specific information. About 250 parents attend the conference each year at the college and know that their role is to bring back information to other parents in their district. Each school district arranges transportation for the parents.

Guidelines for Working With Parents in Changing Suburban Schools

The ultimate goal of parent programming is to get parents engaged and involved in the schools so that they are better equipped to support their children's education. Four guidelines are offered for cultivating successful parent partnerships.

Understand, Acknowledge, and Address Parents' Issues and Challenges

A prevalent theme discussed in this chapter is to acknowledge, understand, and empathize with parent issues and challenges. An understanding of these issues and challenges helps enrich communication and outreach efforts to parents. Figure 8.1 lists major issues and challenges and summarizes ways in which school districts and the community are addressing them.

> **Guidelines for Working With Parents in Changing Suburban Schools**
>
> - Understand, acknowledge, and address parents' issues and challenges
> - Ensure that teachers are knowledgeable about parent challenges
> - Develop collaborative relationships with the community
> - Document success

Ensure That Teachers Are Knowledgeable About Parent Challenges

School leaders need to encourage *all* teachers to support parents. They need to communicate this message in public forums and private conversations and provide workshops and training sessions to help teachers work effectively with parents.

Figure 8.1   Changing Suburbs Solutions to Overcome Parent Challenges

Issue/Challenge	Solution	Entities Involved
Getting parents engaged	• School as center of community and needs based • School as welcoming, supportive culture • School acknowledges and supports parents' needs • Neighborhood outreach in native language • Informal, social programs • New parent engagement by parent	• Schools • College programs • Newcomer Centers • Community organizations
Language	• All outreach in native language • Bilingual website resources and forms • Bilingual counselors and psychologists • Translation services for teachers and staff • Workshops and training in native language	• School districts • College programs • Community organizations
Quality of school's communication	• Bilingual website information • Bilingual in-school resources for translation • Bilingual teacher meetings • Flyers placed in community • Parent discussion groups	• School outreach coordinators • Community organizations
Lack of parent education	• After-school workshops (in native language) to address literacy and other skills • First Steps Early Literacy Program (Ossining) • Parent University (New Rochelle) • Parenting and learning skills (Port Chester) • College leadership and advocacy programs	• Teachers • College programs • Community organizations
Work demands	• School disseminates information in native language that it is easy to share in neighborhoods • Family programs accommodate various schedules and child care	• School districts • Community organizations

Lack of under-standing of school policies and legal rights	• Accessible and bilingual resources and information • Immigration support • Information from the state level • Partnerships provide needed information • Special education workshops	• School districts • College programs • Community organizations
Socioeconomic status/poverty	• Approach the many issues that stem from poverty in a holistic manner to address the healthy development and learning of the child • School as center of community • Multicultural classroom approaches	• School districts • Community organizations
Fear of establish-ment, trust, dis-crimination and attitude of American culture	• Empathetic school personnel • Bilingual resources • District leadership policy and action • Informal, social programs	• School districts • College programs
Feeling intimi-dated by teachers and administrators	• Positive word of mouth by parents • Needs-based school programs • Empathetic school personnel • Bilingual resources/translation	• School districts

Teachers are for the most part the primary contact that parents have with the schools. Teachers often interpret lack of parent involvement as lack of interest. Once teachers are educated about parent challenges and the behaviors that manifest as a result, teachers are able to communicate differently and provide resources to encourage parent involvement in the classroom.

Develop Collaborative Relationships With the Community

Community organizations, such as nonprofit groups, government agencies, and higher-education institutions, can provide additional support and augment the efforts of the schools. Schools can benefit by collaborating with a community organization that has a strong immigrant welcome center, strong outreach, and existing parent groups.

Another form of collaboration is a parent planning committee. This committee should be made up of representatives from the schools and different community organizations to harness resources and to develop and plan parent programs. Such a committee should incorporate information and a variety of perspectives on parent needs and provide input and guidance for a parent leadership program.

Document Success

Use available data to document the success of program initiatives with parents. Word-of-mouth feedback provides anecdotal evidence of parents' responses to different types of outreach and programming. For example, parents still talk about a workshop they attended a few years ago at the college's Hispanic Parents Leadership Institute about helping their children prepare for college. A Hispanic presenter told parents that applying to college is like an enchilada; children must have many ingredients in their portfolio, such as strong academic performance, sports, and other activities. This type of feedback can come from individuals or groups and can help plan for future initiatives and events. Program attendance at conferences and workshops communicates the level of interest and availability of parents, which then helps to plan for future events. Evaluation forms provide written documentation from parents about the perceived effectiveness of different types of programs. These forms can be used to solicit additional ideas from parents about the efficacy of programs. Documented and ongoing evaluation measures success and provides longitudinal evidence for grants.

Concluding Remarks

The African proverb "it takes a village to raise a child," made famous by Hillary Rodham Clinton (1996), appropriately reflects the importance of the cultivation and sustainability of parent partnerships with schools. Many families have undergone tremendous and difficult transitions in moving to a new country, and other families have general economic, work-related, and social pressures. Parents need programs that provide information, offer networking opportunities, and honor and acknowledge their many issues and challenges. School leaders need to leverage the resources, information, and expertise from their own districts and others to help parents become engaged with the schools so that their children have a fighting chance at succeeding in school.

Summary of Guidelines for School Leaders

Although the topics presented in this book could apply to school leaders in general, they bring to the forefront the need for suburban school leaders to adopt a new mind-set and new strategies for the way in which they work with their administrative colleagues, faculty, parents, and community to educate their changing student population. From getting in touch with one's own community to addressing the many components of running a school or school district, this book was written to offer practical and useful ideas that come from our own and other suburban school leaders' firsthand experiences in changing suburban schools.

We provide below *all* the guidelines across the chapters to help school leaders develop new strategies for effecting change in different types of suburban school district organizations.

As school leaders find themselves in schools and districts that are changing, they should:

- Study their community's demographics
- Form networks with like-minded and similarly situated administrators
- Learn about programs that exist and are working in similar schools and districts
- Create a culture of acceptance that communicates to students, their parents, and the community—that the increasingly diverse student population is a welcome addition

As school leaders self-reflect about their own roles and responsibilities, they should:

- Assess their own belief systems in relation to leading changing schools and districts to help with their credibility and vision
- Engage in environmental scans to understand the strengths, weaknesses, opportunities, and threats of a changing population in order to help plan
- Reaffirm existing relationships in their schools and communities, and form new ones to help accomplish goals
- Collaboratively develop a plan of action with short- and long-range goals for a changing student population
- Monitor progress to determine the plan's validity and reliability

As school leaders study and change the culture of their schools and districts, they should:

- Develop self-reflective practices in themselves and others to document and address successes and challenges
- Work within and across cultures to promote an awareness and appreciation of similarities and differences
- Promote oral and written communication practices that support the languages spoken in the school
- Assess a school's climate and culture through multiple mechanisms

As school leaders establish conditions for teachers' professional development, they should:

- Create and articulate a shared vision with teachers
- Create a schoolwide action plan to carry out the shared vision
- Form different teams to move the plan forward
- Articulate clearly the roles and responsibilities of coaches in promoting professional development

As school leaders determine the programs and services to provide for English language learners (ELL) and their families, they should:

- Determine instruction in relation to student needs
- Delineate the roles and responsibilities of school leaders and teachers with different programs and services
- Promote positive interaction in the school and community

As school leaders consider the idea of forming school–university partnerships to help with teachers' professional development and students' achievement, they should:

- Put liaisons in place that most likely can be funded by a neighboring college or university
- Ensure communication among stakeholders
- Have written agreements to lay out the purpose of the partnership, roles and responsibilities of partners, any financial arrangements, and intended duration
- Make sure funding is available to support the partnership's mission
- Assess the partnership's viability to determine ways to strengthen different initiatives

As school leaders consider the idea of developing community schools to bring resources to their schools and help their immigrant populations, they should:

- Embrace and promote the community school concept
- Encourage teachers to open their classrooms to community partners
- Help partners to support their schools as well as their community

As school leaders discover ways to involve minority and immigrant parents in their schools, they should:

- Understand, acknowledge, and address parents' issues and challenges
- Ensure that teachers are knowledgeable about parent challenges
- Develop collaborative relationships with the community
- Document success

Change is not easy, especially when it affects the status quo in demanding ways. Suburban school leaders, intent on being responsive to all of their stakeholders as they grapple with statewide and national mandates, are responsible for managing this change. Suburban school leaders know that there are no quick fixes to the myriad of challenges that accompany a changing student population with achievement, language, and poverty pressures.

School leaders need to take a step back to first study the changes in their schools and districts, and then work with their respective stakeholders to create a viable, supportive, and successful culture for meeting diverse students' needs, especially those whose first language is not English and those who are new immigrants to the United States. We recognize that, as suburban school leaders do their due diligence in orchestrating new ways of using resources to accommodate these dramatic changes, they also need others within and outside their communities—legislators, politicians, and business executives—to pay more attention to the needs of the changing suburbs. The time, attention, and resources that usually are given to urban educational systems now should be given to suburban educational systems as well, if we truly believe in *success for all.* To borrow from Bob Dylan, "Come senators, congressmen, please heed the call, that the *suburbs* they are a changin.'"

References

Alba, R., Logan, J., Stults, B. J., Marzan, G., & Zhang, W. (1999). Immigrant groups and suburbs: A re-examination of suburbanization and spatial assimilation. *American Sociological Review, 64*(3), 446–460.

Allington, R. (2006). *What really matters for struggling readers: Designing research based programs.* Boston, MA: Pearson Allyn and Bacon.

Angelou, M. (1993). *Wouldn't take nothing for my journey now.* New York, NY: Random House.

Anonymous. (n.d.). Diversity quote. Retrieved from http://www.icelebrate diversity.com/CorporateDiversity/diversity_quotes.htm

Badlow, R. (2001). Suburban bigotry: A descent into racism and struggle for redemption. *Multicultural Education, 8*(3), 15–17.

Baker, C. (2011). *Foundations of bilingual education and bilingualism* (5th ed.). Clevedon, UK: Multilingual Matters.

Banks, J. A. (2001). Citizenship education and diversity: Implications for teacher education. *Journal of Teacher Education, 52*(1), 5–16.

Banks, J. A. (2004). Teaching for social justice, diversity, and citizenship in a global world. *The Educational Forum, 68,* 296–305.

Banks, J., Cochran-Smith, M., Moll, L., Richert, A., Zeichner, K., LePage, P., Darling-Hammond, L., Duffy, H., with McDonald, M. (2005). Teaching diverse learners. In L. Darling-Hammond, J. Bransford, P. LePage, K. Hammerness, & H. Duffy (Eds.), *Preparing teachers for a changing world: What teachers should learn and be able to do* (pp. 232–274). San Francisco, CA: Jossey-Bass.

Bean, R. M., Draper, J. A., Hall, V., Vandermolen, J., & Zigmond, N. (2010). Coaches and coaching in reading first schools: A reality check. *Elementary School Journal, 111*(1), 87–114.

Beavers, J. M. (2006). *Developmental reading assessment, K–3* (2nd ed.). Retrieved from http://www.sedl.org/cgi-bin/mysql/rad.cgi?searchid=230

Bell, C., & Newby, H. (1974). *The sociology of community: A selection of readings.* London: Frank Cass.

Bernstein, M. F. (2004, July 25). The urbanization of suburban classrooms. *The New York Times,* pp. 1–2. Retrieved from http://www.nytimes.com

Biancarosa, G., Bryk, A. S., & Dexter, E. R. (2010). Assessing the value-added effects of literacy collaborative professional development on student learning. *Elementary School Journal, 111*(1), 7–34.

Bishop, R. S. (1990). Mirrors, windows, and sliding glass doors. *Perspectives: Choosing and using books for the classroom, 6*(3), ix–xi.

Blank, M. J., Jacobson, R., Melaville, A., & Pearson, S. (2010). *Financing community schools: Leveraging resources to support student success.* Washington, DC: Coalition for Community Schools.

Boles, K. C. (1992, April). *School restructuring by teachers: A study of the teaching project at the Edward Devotion School.* Paper presented at the annual meeting of the American Educational Research Association, San Francisco, CA.

Borthwick, A. C., Stirling, T., Nauman, A. D., & Cook, D. L. (2003). Achieving successful school–university collaboration. *Urban Education, 38(3)*, 330–371.

Boystown. (n.d.). *The common sense parenting.* Retrieved from http://www .boystown.org/new-england/news/new-common-sense-parenting -classes-bring-families-together

Brown, J. E., & Doolittle, J. (2008). *A cultural, linguistical, and ecological framework for response to intervention with English language learners.* National Center for Culturally Responsible Educational Systems. Retrieved from http://nccrest.org/Briefs/Framework_for_RTI.pdf

Browne-Ferrigno, T., & Allen, L. W. (2006). Preparing principals for high-need rural schools: A central office perspective about collaborative efforts to transform school leadership. *Journal of Research in Rural Education, 21*(1), 1–16.

Bruno, M. (2010, October 7). *U-46 to expand dual language program.* Retrieved from mysuburbanlife.com

Budge, K. (2006, December 18). Rural leaders, rural places: Problem, privilege, and possibility. *Journal of Research in Rural Education, 21*(13). Retrieved from http://jrre.psu.edu/articles/21-13.pdf

Bullough, R. V., & Baughman, K. (1997). *"First year teacher" eight years later: An inquiry into teacher development.* New York, NY: Teachers College Press.

Burris, C. C., & Welner, K. G. (2005). Closing the achievement gap by detracking. *Phi Delta Kappan, 86*(8), 594–598.

Butrymowicz, S. (2011, March 15). Connecticut's achievement gap not just an inner city issue. *The Hechinger Report.* Retrieved from http://www.ctmirror .org/story/11721/connecticuts-achievement-persists-every-district

Byrd, D. M., & McIntryre, D. J. (2011). Types of partnerships. In S. B. Wepner & D. Hopkins (Eds.), *Collaborative leadership in action: Partnering for success in schools* (pp. 27–48). New York, NY: Teachers College Press.

Cabrera, R. (2011, Agosto/Septiembre). ABCD . . . ¡Español! *Siempre Mujer*, 94–98.

Calderón, M. E., & Minaya-Rowe, L. (2003). *Designing and implementing two-way bilingual programs.* Thousand Oaks, CA: Corwin.

Carrasquillo, A. L., & Rodriquez, V. (2006). *Language minority student in the mainstream classroom* (2nd ed.). Philadelphia, PA: Multilingual Matters.

Castle, S., Rockwood, K. D., & Tortora, M. (2008). Tracking professional development and student learning in a professional development school partnership. *School–University Partnerships: The Journal of the National Association for Professional Development Schools, 2*(1), 47–60.

The Children's Aid Society. (2001). *Building a community school* (3rd ed.). New York, NY: Author.

Clark, R. M. (1990). Why disadvantaged children succeed: What happens outside of school is critical. *Public Welfare, 48*(2), 17–23. Retrieved from http://www.aphsa.org

Clark, R. W. (1999). *Effective professional development schools.* San Francisco, CA: Jossey-Bass.

Clinton, H. R. (1996). *It takes a village: And other lessons children teach us.* New York, NY: Simon & Schuster.

Collier, V. P. (1987). Age and rate of acquisition of second language for academic purposes. *TESOL Quarterly, 21,* 617–641.

Collier, V. P., & Thomas, W. P. (2004). The astounding effectiveness of dual language education for all. *NABE Journal of Research and Practice, 2*(1), 1–20.

Collier, V. P., & Thomas, W. P. (2009). *Educating English language learners for a transformed world.* Albuquerque: Dual Language Education of New Mexico Fuente Press.

Cool Avenues. (n.d.). *Marketing glossary: Environmental scanning.* Retrieved from http://coolavenues.com/know/mktg/ee.php3

Cotton, K. (2000). *The schooling practices that matter most.* Retrieved from http://www.nwrel.org/scpd/sirs/31cu6.html

Crow, G. M. (2006). Complexity and the beginning principal in the United States: Perspectives on socialization. *Journal of Educational Administration, 44*(4), 310–325.

Cummins, J. (1984). *Bilingualism and special education: Issues in assessment and pedagogy.* San Diego, CA: College-Hill Press.

Cummins, J. (2001). *Negotiating identities: Education for empowerment in a diverse society* (2nd ed.). Los Angeles: California Association for Bilingual Education.

Dabbah, M. (2006). *Ayude a sus hijos a tener éxito en la escuela: Guía para padres Latinos.* Naperville, IL: Sphinx Pub.

Dana, N. F., Tricarico, K., & Quinn, D. (2010). The administrator as action researcher: A case study of five principals and their engagement in systematic, intentional study of their own practice. *Journal of School Leadership, 19*(3), 232–265.

Danielson, C. (1999). Mentoring beginning teachers: The case for mentoring. *Teaching and Change, 6*(3), 251–257.

Daresh, J. C. (2003). *Teachers mentoring teachers: A practical approach to helping new and experienced staff.* Thousand Oaks, CA: Corwin.

Daresh, J. C., & Aplin, N. D. (2001). Educational leadership and the suburban superintendent. *Education, 107*(4), 209–218.

Dauber, S., & Epstein, J. (1993). Parents' attributes and practices of involvement in inner-city elementary and middle schools. In N. F. Chavkin (Ed.), *Family and schools in a pluralistic society* (pp. 53–72). Albany: State University of New York Press.

Davis, B. G. (2009). *Tools for teaching* (2nd ed.). San Francisco, CA: Jossey-Bass.

Denton, N. A., Hernandez, D. J., & Macartney, S. E. (2009). School-age children in immigrant families: Challenges and opportunities for America's schools. *Teachers College Record, 111*(3), 615–658.

Dillon, M. (2011, June). Mapping suburban school reform. *American School Board Journal.* Retrieved from http://www.asbj.com/TopicsArchive/Leadership/Mapping-Suburban-School-Reform.html

Dole, J. A. (2004). The changing role of the reading specialist in school reform. *The Reading Teacher, 57*(5), 462–471.

Downey, J. A., & Cobbs, G. A. (2007). I actually learned a lot from this: A field assignment to prepare future preservice math teachers for culturally diverse classrooms. *School Science and Mathematics, 107*(1), 391–403.

Drago-Severson, E. (2004). *Helping teachers learn. Principal leadership for adult growth and development.* Thousand Oaks, CA: Corwin.

Dryfoos, J. G. (1998). *Safe passages: Making it through adolescence in a risky society.* New York, NY: Oxford University Press.

Dudley-Marling, C. (2007). Return of the deficit. *Journal of Educational Controversy, 2*(1). Retrieved from http://www.wce.wwu.edu/resources/cep/ejournal/v002n001/a004.shtml

Duffield, J. A., & Cates, W. M. (2008). Establishing and maintaining professional development schools: A delphi study. *School–University Partnerships: The Journal of the National Association for Professional Development Schools, 2*(2), 27–50.

Dyson, L. L. (1999). Developing a university–school district partnership: Researcher–district administrator collaboration for a special education initiative. *Canadian Journal of Education, 24*(4), 411–425.

Echevarría, J., & Vogt, M. (2011). *Response to Intervention (RTI) and English learners: Making it happen.* Boston, MA: Pearson.

Echevarría, J., Vogt, M., & Short, D. J. (2008). *Making content comprehensible for English learners: The SIOP model.* Boston, MA: Pearson Allyn and Bacon.

Education and the New Latino Diaspora. (2011, Summer). *Penn GSE,* pp. 6–7, 14–15.

Environmental scanning. (n.d.). Retrieved from http://en.wikipedia.org/wiki/Environmental_scanning

Erwin, S., Winn, P., Gentry, J., & Cauble, M. (2010, April). *A comparison of urban, suburban, and rural principal leadership skills by campus student achievement level.* Proceedings of the Annual Meeting of the American Educational Research Association SIG: Leadership for school improvement, Denver, CO.

Estrada, V. L., Gómez, L., & Ruiz-Escalante, J. A. (2009). Let's make dual language the norm. *Educational Leadership, 66*(7), 54–68.

Evans, A. (2007). Changing faces: Suburban school response to demographic change. *Education and Urban Society, 39*(3), 315–348.

Ferrara, J., & Santiago, E. (2007). Crossroads: Where community meets character in the pursuit of academic excellence. *The Journal of Research in Character Education, 5*(1), 95–101.

Fessenden, F. (2007, September 16). Suburbs gaining Asians and Hispanics. *The New York Times.* Retrieved from http://www.nytimes.com

Fry, R. (2007). The changing race and ethnic composition of U.S. public schools. *Pew Hispanic Center.* Retrieved from http://pewhispanic.org/reports/report.php?ReportID=79

Fry, R., & Gonzales, F. (2008). One-in-five and growing fast: A profile of Hispanic public school students. *Pew Hispanic Center.* Retrieved from http://pewhispanic.org/reports/report.php?ReportID=92

Gangi, J. M. (2008). The unbearable whiteness of literacy instruction: Realizing the implications of the proficient reader research. *Multicultural Review, 17*(2), 30–35.

Gardner, J. W. (1968). No easy victories. *The American Statistician, 22*(1), 14–16.

Garnett, N. S. (2007). Suburbs as exit, suburbs as entrance. *Michigan Law Review, 106*(2), 277–304.

Gee, J. P. (2004). *Situated language and learning: A critique of traditional schooling.* New York, NY: Routledge.

Gentle, E. (2011, January 25). City of Huntsville hires demographer to help city school situation. *48 News.* Retrieved from http://www.waff.com/story/13906697/city-of-huntsville-hires-demographer-to-help-city-school-situation

Giouroukakis,V., Cohan, A., Nenchin, J., & Honigsfeld, A. (2011). A second set of eyes and ears: Observation protocol boosts skills for teachers of ELL students. *JSD, 32*(3), 60–63.

Gómez, D. W., Ferrara, J., Santiago, E., Fanelli, F., & Taylor, R. (2012). Full-service community schools: A district's commitment to educating the whole child. In A. Honigsfeld & A. Cohan (Eds.), *Breaking the mold of education for culturally and linguistically diverse students: Innovative and successful practices for the 21st century* (pp. 65–73). Lanham, MD: Rowman & Littlefield Education.

Gómez, D. W., Lang, D. E., & Lasser, S. M. (2010). *Nuevas avenidas:* Pathways for modeling and supporting home-based literacy strategies with Hispanic parents. In A. Honigsfeld & A. Cohan (Eds.), *Breaking the mold of school instruction and organization: Innovative and successful practices for the 21st century* (pp. 123–128). Lanham, MD: Rowman & Littlefield Education.

Goodwin, A. L. (2002). Teacher preparation and the education of immigrant children. *Education and Urban Society, 34*(2), 156–172.

Graham, R. (2010). PIQE graduates find that knowledge is power–for parents and children. *The Memorial Examiner.* Retrieved from http://www

.yourhoustonnews.com/memorial/news/article_91e53527-1967-5ea()
-97f5-5d11125aa5b8.html?mode=image

Greene, P., & Tichenor, M. (1999). Partnerships on a collaborative continuum. *Contemporary Education, 70*(4), 13–19.

Harris, D. R. (1999, September). *All suburbs are not created equal: A new look at racial differences in suburban location.* (Report No. 99-440). Ann Arbor: University of Michigan, Population Studies Center at the Institute for Social Research University.

Heath, S. B. (1983). *Ways with words: Language, life, and work in communities and classrooms.* Cambridge, MA: Cambridge University Press.

Heifetz, R. A. (1994). *Leadership without easy answers.* Cambridge, MA: Harvard University Press.

Henderson, A. T., & Berla, N. (1994). *A new generation of evidence: The family is critical to student achievement.* Retrieved from http://eric.ed.gov (ED375968)

The history of settlement houses. (n.d.). In *Jacob A. Riis neighborhood settlement houses.* Retrieved from http://www.riissettlement.org/index2/htm

Hochman, J. (2009, September). *"State of the District" report to the Board of Education.* Unpublished report.

Hoover-Dempsey, K. V., & Sandler, H. M. (2005). *Final performance report for OERI Grant #R305T010673: The social context of parental involvement: A path to enhanced achievement.* Retrieved from http://www.vanderbilt.edu/peabody/family-school/Reports.html

Hord, S. M. (1997). Professional learning communities: What are they and why are they important? *Issues About Change, 6*(1), 1–8.

Houston, W. R., Hollis, L. Y., Clay, D., Ligons, C. M., & Roff, L. (1999). Effects of collaboration on urban teacher education programs and professional development schools. In D. M. Byrd & D. J. McIntyre (Eds.), *Research on professional development schools. Teacher Education Yearbook VII* (pp. 6–28). Thousand Oaks, CA: Corwin.

Houts, P. L. (1976). A principal and his school: A conversation with Roland Barth. *The National Elementary Principal, 56*(2), 8–21.

Howard, G. (2007). As diversity grows, so must we. *Educational Leadership, 64*(6), 16–22.

Howley, C. B., Howley, A., & Larson, W. (1999). Do rural and suburban principals approach planning differently? A two-state comparison. *Journal of Research in Rural Education, 15*(3), 165–180.

Hwang, S., & Murdock, S. H. (1998). Racial attraction or racial avoidance in American suburbs? *Social Forces, 77*(2), 541–566.

Iacocca, L. (2007). *Where have all the leaders gone?* New York, NY: Scribner.

Immigrate to Manitoba, Canada. (n.d.). *Immigration planning guide: Conduct an internal and external environmental scan.* Retrieved from http://www2.immigratemanitoba.com/browse/regionalcommunities/plan_guide/community-int_ext.html

The impact of parental involvement in children's education. (2008). Retrieved from http://www.northlincs.gov.uk/NR/rdonlyres/5C39FCD7-8075-40FD-9A08-06614F4FEB1D/14909/TheImpactofParentalInvolvementon365kb2.pdf

Jones, S. (2006). *Girls, social class, and literacy: What teachers can do to make a difference.* Portsmouth, NH: Heinemann.

Kegan, R. (2000). What "form" transforms? A constructive-developmental approach to transformative learning. In J. Mezirow & Associates (Eds.), *Learning as transformation* (pp. 35–70). San Francisco, CA: Jossey-Bass.

Kendell, D. (2009, April). The basic do-and-reflect experiential model. *The Effective Leadership Development Community.* Retrieved from http://effective.leadershipdevelopment.edu.au/basic-reflect-experiential-model/active-learning/

KewalRamani, A., Gilbertson, L., Fox, M., & Provasnik, S. (2007). *Status and trends in the education of racial and ethnic minorities.* Retrieved from http://nces.ed.gov/pubs2007/2007039.pdf

Killion, J. (2000). Exemplary schools model quality staff development. *Results,* p. 3.

Labov, W. (1972). *The language of the inner city.* Philadelphia: University of Pennsylvania Press.

Ladson-Billings, G. (2006). From the achievement gap to the education debt: Understanding achievement in U.S. schools. *Educational Researcher, 35*(7), 3–12.

Lang, D. E., Gómez, D. W., & Lasser, S. M. (2009). *Preparados, listos, ya!:* An interpretative case study centered on teaching Hispanic parents to support early bilingual literacy development prior to kindergarten. *GiST (Revista Colombiana de Educacion Bilingüe/Colombian Journal of Bilingual Education), 3,* 90–106.

Lang, D. E., & Siry, C. (August, 2008). Diversity as a context for inquiry-based pre-service teacher learning and teaching in elementary school settings: A self-study in teacher education practices. In M. L. Heston, D. L. Tidwell, K. East, & L. M. Fitzgerald (Eds.), *Pathways to change in teacher education: Dialogue, diversity and self-study proceedings from the seventh international conference on self-study of teacher education practices* (pp. 213–217). Cedar Falls: University of Northern Iowa.

Lareau, A. (1989). *Home advantage: Social class and parental intervention in elementary education.* New York, NY: Falmer Press.

Leverett, L. (2011, April). The urban superintendents program leadership framework. In R. Peterkin, D. Jewell-Sherman, L. Kelley, & L. Boozer (Eds.), *Every child, every classroom, every day: School leaders who are making equity a reality* (pp. 1–15). San Francisco, CA: Jossey-Bass.

Lewin, K. (1946). Action research and minority problems. *Journal of Social Issues, 2*(4), 34–46.

Lindquist, T. (2002). *Seeing the whole through social studies* (2nd ed.). Portsmouth, NH: Heinemann.

Lindsey, J. (2011, June 29). Bates named superintendent. *The Daily Admoreite.* Retrieved from http://www.ardmoreite.com/features/x2108624818/ Bates-named-superintendent

Lopez, M. H. (2009). *Latinos and education: Explaining the attainment gap.* Retrieved from http://pewhispanic.org/reports/report.php?ReportID=115

Louis, K. S. (2003). School leaders facing real change: Shifting geography, uncertain paths. *Cambridge Journal of Education, 33*(3), 371–382.

Loveland, E. (2002). Challenges and rewards of rural school leadership. *The rural school and community trust, 3*(6), 1–9.

Lowery, S., & Harris, S. (2002). The Blytheville story: The challenge of changing demographics. *Journal of Cases in Educational Leadership, 5*(3), 49–55.

Lutton, L. (2009, December 15). Shifting demographics change suburban schools. *Chicago Public Media/WBEZ91.5.* Retrieved from http://www .wbez.org/story/shifting-demographics-change-suburban-schools#

Maker, G. (2010). BOE candidates call for parental involvement in school district. *The Report: The New Rochelle Sound & Town Report.* Retrieved from http://mysoundreport.com/index.php?option=com_content&view =articel&id=700:boe-candidates-call-for-parental-involvment-in-school-district&catid=35:news&itemdid=53

Martin, M., Fergus, E., & Noguera, P. (2010). Responding to the needs of the whole child: A case study of a high-performing elementary school for immigrant children. *Reading & Writing Quarterly, 26*(3), 195–222.

Matsumura, L. C., Garnier, H. E., Correnti, R., Junker, B., & Bickel, D. D. (2010). Investigating the effectiveness of a comprehensive literacy coaching program in schools with high teacher mobility. *The Elementary School Journal, 111*(1), 35–62.

McIntosh, P. (1988). *White privilege: Unpacking the invisible knapsack.* Wellesley, MA: Wellesley College Center for Research on Women. Retrieved from http://nymbp.org/reference/WhitePrivilege.pdf

McKeon, D. (2004). When meeting "common" standards is uncommonly difficult. *Educational Leadership, 51*(8), 45–49.

Mead, M. (1935). *Sex and temperament in three primitive societies.* New York, NY: William Morrow.

Miles, K. H., & Hornbeck, M. (2000). *Reinvesting in teachers: Aligning district professional development spending to support a comprehensive school reform strategy.* District Issues Brief. Washington, DC: New American Schools.

Miller, L. J. (1995). Family togetherness and the suburban idea. *Sociological Forum, 10*(3), 393–418.

Moir, E., & Bloom, G. (2003). Fostering leadership through mentoring. *Educational Leadership, 60*(8), 58–60.

Moll, L. C., Amanti, C., Neff, D., & Gonzalez, N. (1992). Funds of knowledge for teaching: Using a qualitative approach to connect homes and classrooms. *Theory Into Practice, 31*(1), 132–141.

Moreno, N. (2005, Spring). Science education partnerships: Being realistic about meeting expectations. *Cell Biology Education, 4*(1), 30–32.

Moss, L. (n.d.). Importance of school demographics to success. Retrieved from http://www.ehow.com/facts_6141539_importance-school-demographics -success.html

National Center on Response to Intervention. (2011, August). *RTI consider- ations for English Language Learners (ELLs).* Washington, DC: U.S. Department of Education. Retrieved from http://www.rti4success.org/ pdf/0728%20RTI%20ELL%20Summary%20d4.pdf

National Commission on Teaching and America's Future. (1996). *What matters most: Teaching for America's future.* New York, NY: Author.

National Commission on Teaching and America's Future. (1997). *Doing what matters most: Investing in quality teaching.* New York, NY: Author.

National Council for the Social Studies. (2010). *National curriculum standards for social studies: A framework for teaching, learning, and assessment.* Waldorf, MD: Author.

The Netter Center for Community Partnerships: University of Pennsylvania. (n.d.). *University-assisted community schools mission & Penn-Sayre high school partnerships.* Philadelphia, PA: Author.

The New York City Department of Education. (2011). Our community. In *P.S. 005 Ellen Lurie.* Retrieved from http://schools.nyc.gov/SchoolPortals/06/ M005/AboutUs/Overview/Our+Community.htm

Nicolau, S., & Ramos, C. (1990). *Together is better: Building strong relationships between schools and Hispanic parents.* Retrieved from http://eric.ed.gov (ED325543)

Nieto, S. (2009). *Language, culture, and teaching: Critical perspectives.* New York, NY: Routledge.

Nieto, S. (2010). *The light in their eyes: Creating mulitcultural learning communi- ties.* New York, NY: Teachers College Press.

Noguera, P. (2007, July 29). Closing the racial achievement gap: The best strat- egies of the schools we send them to. *In Motion Magazine.* Retrieved from http://www.inmotionmagazine.com/er/pn_strat.html

Obama, M. (2009, May 18). *Remarks at the American Ballet opening spring gala.* Retrieved from http://teachingthroughthearts.blogspot.com/ 2009_06_01_archive.html

Olson, L. (1987, March 18). Goodlad seeks stronger school–university alli- ances. *Education Week.* Retrieved from http://www.edweek.org/ew/ articles/1987/03/18/2525netw.h06.html

Parent Institute for Quality Education. (2010). *Parent engagement education program: A process of parent empowerment.* Retrieved from http://www .piqe.org/prog_parentengage.php

Child Trends Data Bank. (2010). *Parent involvement in schools.* Retrieved from http://www.childtrendsdatabank.org/?q=node/186

Pashiardis, P. (1996). Environmental scanning in educational organizations: Uses, approaches, sources and methodologies. *International Journal of Educational Management, 10*(3), 5–9.

Peel, H. A., Peel, B. B., & Baker, M. E. (2002). School–university partnerships: A viable model. *The International Journal of Educational Management, 16*(7), 319–325.

Popovics, A. J. (1990). Environmental scanning: A process to assist colleges in strategic planning. *College Student Journal, 24,* 78–80.

Portin, B. S. (2000). The changing urban principalship. *Education and urban society, 32*(4), 492–505.

Press, E. (2007). The new suburban poverty. *The Nation.* Retrieved from http://www.thenation.com/article/new-suburban-poverty

Rainville, K. N., & Jones, S. (2008). Situated identities: Power and positioning in the work of a literacy coach. *The Reading Teacher, 61*(6), 440–448.

Rector, R. (2006). Importing poverty: Immigration and poverty in the United States: A book of charts. *The Heritage Special Report.* Retrieved from http://thf_media.s3.amazonaws.com/2006/pdf/sr9.pdf

Richard, A. (2000). Remodeling suburbia: 2000 and beyond: The changing face of American schools. *Education Week, 2*(7). Retrieved from http://www.edweek.org

Rong, X. L., & Preissle, J. (2009). *Educating immigrant students in the 21st century: What educators need to know.* Thousand Oaks, CA: Corwin.

Roscigno, V. J., Tomaskovic-Devey, D., & Crowley, M. L. (2006). Education and the inequalities of place. *Social Forces, 84*(4), 2121–2145.

Rothstein-Fisch, C., & Trumbull, E. (2008). *Managing diverse classrooms: How to build on students' cultural strengths.* Alexandria, VA: Association for Supervision and Curriculum Development.

Rothstein, A. L. (2001). A college goes to school: The history of an urban collaboration. *Education, 122*(2), 231–239.

Rowley, J. B. (1999). The good mentor. *Educational Leadership, 56*(8), 20–22.

Salend, S. J., & Salinas, A. (2003). Language differences or learning difficulties: The work of the multidisciplinary team. *Teaching Exceptional Children, 35*(40), 36–43.

Santiago, E., Ferrara, J., & Quinn, J. (in press). *Whole child, whole school: Applying theory to practice in a community school.* Lanham, MD: Rowman & Littlefield Education.

School–college joint efforts said to remain elusive. (1989, March 15). *Education Week.* Retrieved from http://www.edweek.org/ew/articles/1989/03/15/08210005.h08.html

Schools Uniting Neighborhoods. (2003). *Successful collaboration in an environment of change.* Portland, OR: Author.

Sergiovanni, T. (1999). *Building community in schools.* San Francisco, CA: Jossey-Bass.

Sergiovanni, T. (2009). *The principalship: A reflective practice perspective.* Boston, MA: Allyn and Bacon.

Shannon, G. S., & Bylsma, P. (2007). *The nine characteristics of high-performing schools: A research-based resource for schools and districts to assist with improving student learning.* (2nd ed.). Olympia, WA: Office of Superintendent of Public Instruction.

Sharp, K. (2003, Summer). Teacher reflection: A perspective from the trenches. *Theory Into Practice, (42)*3, 243–247.

Siry, C., & Lang, D. E. (2010). How will I know when you've got it? Creating participatory discourse for teaching and research in early childhood science. *Journal of Science Teacher Education, 21*(2), 149–160.

Smith, J., Stern, K., & Shatrova, Z. (2008). Factors inhibiting Hispanic parents' school involvement. *Rural Educator, 29*(2), 8–13.

Sobel, A., & Kugler, E. G. (2007). Building partnerships with immigrant parents. *Responding to Changing Demographics, 64*(6), 62–66.

Speck, M. (1996, Spring). Best practice in professional development for sustained educational change. *ERS Spectrum,* 33–41.

Stroble, B., & Luka, H. (1999). It's my life now: The impact of professional development school partnerships on university and school administrators. *Peabody Journal of Education, 74*(4), 123–135.

The suburban challenge. (2009, January 17). *Newsweek,* Retrieved from http://www.newsweek.com/

Suro, R. (2007). The Hispanic family in flux. *Center on Children and Families Working Paper in collaboration with the Annie E. Casey Foundation.* Retrieved from http://www.brookings.edu/~/media/Files/rc/papers/2007/11_hispanicfamily_suro/11_hispanicfamily_suro.pdf

Sykes, G. (1996). Reform of and as professional development. *Phi Delta Kappan, 77*(7), 465–467.

Teaching Tolerance. (2010). *Introduction to culturally relevant pedadogy.* Retrieved from http://www.youtube.com/watch?v=nGTVjJuRaZ8

Tillman, T. (2007). *Healthy neighborhoods healthy kids guide.* Burlington, VT: Shelburne Farms' Sustainable Schools Project.

Tomanek, D. (2005, Spring). Building successful partnerships between K–12 and universities. *Cell Biology Education, 4*(1), 28–29.

Treadway, L. (2000). *Community mapping.* Unpublished manuscript. Contextual Teaching and Learning Project, Ohio State University and U.S. Department of Education.

The University of Chicago. (2010, October 7). *Poverty grows in suburbs, but social services don't keep up: Report.* Retrieved from http://www.physorg.com/news205644443.html

University of Cincinnati. (2010, August, 16). *Researchers examine patterns of minority suburbanization circling the nation's major cities.* Retrieved from http://www.physorg.com/news201173727.html

University of Maryland. (2005). Definition of diversity. *Diversity at UMCP: Moving toward community plan 1995.* Retrieved from http://www.inform.umd.edu/EdRes/Topic/Diversity/Reference/diversity.html

U.S. Census Bureau. (2009). *American community survey.* Washington, DC: Author.

U.S. Department of Education, National Center for Education Statistics. (2011). *The condition of education 2011.* (NCES 2011-033, Indicator 6). Retrieved from http://nces.ed.gov/fastfacts/display.asp?id=96

U.S. Department of Justice. (2008, April). *Attorney General's report to Congress on the growth of violent street gangs in suburban areas: Appendix A: Scope and methodology.* Retrieved from http://www.justice.gov/ndic/pubs27/27612/appenda.htm

Valdes, G. (1996). *Con respeto: Bridging the distances between culturally diverse families and schools: An ethnographic portrait.* New York, NY: Teachers College Press.

Valdes, G., Capitelli, S., & Alvarez, L. (2011). *Latino children learning English: Steps in the journey.* New York, NY: Teachers College Press.

Valladolid, D. (2010). *President's message. About us.* Retrieved from http://www.piqe.org/about_pres_msg.php

Vandegrift D., & Yoked T. (2004). Obesity rates, income and suburban sprawl: An analysis of U.S. states. *Health and Place, 10*(3), 221–229.

Vaughn, S., & Ortiz, A. (n.d.). Response to intervention in reading for English language learners. *RTI Action Network.* Retrieved from http://www.rtinetwork.org/learn/diversity/englishlanguagelearners

Walberg, H. J. (1984, February). Families as partners in educational productivity. *Phi Delta Kappan,* 397–400. Retrieved from http://heartland.org/sites/all/modules/custom/heartland_migration/files/pdfs/16032.pdf

Walker, D. A., Downey, P. M., & Cox-Henderson, J. (2010). REAL Camp: A school–university collaboration to promote post-secondary educational opportunities among high school students. *The Educational Forum, 74,* 297–304.

Walker, D. A., Sorensen, C. K., Smaldino, S. E., & Downey, P. (2008). A model for professional development school intervention: REAL findings. *School–University Partnerships, 2*(1), 6–26.

Wepner, S. B. (2011). How to become a collaborative leader. In S. B. Wepner & D. Hopkins (Eds.), *Collaborative leadership in action: Partnering for success in schools* (pp. 166–183). New York, NY: Teachers College Press.

Wepner, S. B., Bettica, A., Gangi, J., Reilly, M. A., & Klemm, T. (2008). Using a cross-curricular learning experience to promote student engagement through a school–college collaboration. *Excelsior, 3*(1), 27–45.

Wepner, S. B., Bowes, K. A., & Serotkin, R. (2007). Technology in teacher education: Creating a climate of change and collaboration. *Action in Teacher Education, 29*(1), 81–93.

Wepner, S. B., Hopkins, D., Johnson, V. C., & Damico, S. (2011, Winter). Emerging characteristics of education deans' collaborative leadership. *Academic Leadership Online Journal, 9*(1). Available from http://www.academicleadership.org/article/emerging-characteristics-of-education-deans-collaborative-leadership

Wepner, S. B., & Tao, L. (2002). From master teacher to master novice: Shifting responsibilities in technology-infused classrooms. *The Reading Teacher, 55*(7), 642–651.

Willis, J. (2011). Making evaluation useful: Improving partnerships through ongoing collaborative assessment. In S. B. Wepner & D. Hopkins (Eds.), *Collaborative leadership in action: Partnering for success in schools* (pp. 97–118). New York, NY: Teachers College Press.

Willis, S. (2002). Creating a knowledge base for teaching: A conversation with James Stigler. *Educational Leadership, 59*(6), 6–11.

Wimpelberg, R. K. (1997). Superintending: The undeniable politics and indefinite effects of school district leadership. *American Journal of Education, 105*(3), 319–345.

Wong-Fillmore, L. (1991). When learning a second language means losing the first. *Early Childhood Research Quarterly, 6,* 323–346.

Yaccino, S. (2010, July, 12*). Poor suburbia: Rethinking the geography of American poverty.* Retrieved from http://www.physorg.com/news198148853.html.

Young, C., & Rasinski, T. (2009). Implementing readers theatre as an approach to classroom fluency instruction. *The Reading Teacher, 63*(1), 4–13.

Zarante, M. E. (2007). Understanding Latino parental involvement in education: Perceptions, expectations, and recommendations. *The Tomas Rivera Policy Institute.* Retrieved from http://ea.niusileadscape.org/docs/FINAL_PRODUCTS/LearningCarousel/LatinoParentalInvolvement.pdf

Index

CORWIN
A SAGE Company

The Corwin logo—a raven striding across an open book—represents the union of courage and learning. Corwin is committed to improving education for all learners by publishing books and other professional development resources for those serving the field of PreK–12 education. By providing practical, hands-on materials, Corwin continues to carry out the promise of its motto: **"Helping Educators Do Their Work Better."**